Samuel French Acting Edition

Thespian Playworks 2018

Placebo
by **Tan'yeasia Brewster**

Stratocumulus
by **Sofia Bottinelli**

Derailed
by **Jared Goudsmit**

Umtya (The String)
by **Frances Louise Timberlake**

Placebo Copyright © 2019 by Tan'yeasia Brewster
Stratocumulus Copyright © 2019 by Sofia Bottinelli
Derailed Copyright © 2019 by Jared Goudsmit
Umtya (The String) Copyright © 2019 by Frances Louise Timberlake
All Rights Reserved

THESPIAN PLAYWORKS 2018 is fully protected under the copyright laws of the United States of America, the British Commonwealth, including Canada, and all member countries of the Berne Convention for the Protection of Literary and Artistic Works, the Universal Copyright Convention, and/or the World Trade Organization conforming to the Agreement on Trade Related Aspects of Intellectual Property Rights. All rights, including professional and amateur stage productions, recitation, lecturing, public reading, motion picture, radio broadcasting, television, online/digital production, and the rights of translation into foreign languages are strictly reserved.

ISBN 978-0-573-70778-0

www.concordtheatricals.com
www.concordtheatricals.co.uk

FOR PRODUCTION INQUIRIES

UNITED STATES AND CANADA
info@concordtheatricals.com
1-866-979-0447

UNITED KINGDOM AND EUROPE
licensing@concordtheatricals.co.uk
020-7054-7200

Each title is subject to availability from Concord Theatricals Corp., depending upon country of performance. Please be aware that *THESPIAN PLAYWORKS 2018* may not be licensed by Concord Theatricals Corp. in your territory. Professional and amateur producers should contact the nearest Concord Theatricals Corp. office or licensing partner to verify availability.

CAUTION: Professional and amateur producers are hereby warned that *THESPIAN PLAYWORKS 2018* is subject to a licensing fee. The purchase, renting, lending or use of this book does not constitute a license to perform this title(s), which license must be obtained from Concord Theatricals Corp. prior to any performance. Performance of this title(s) without a license is a violation of federal law and may subject the producer and/or presenter of such performances to civil penalties. Both amateurs and professionals considering a production are strongly advised to apply to the appropriate agent before starting rehearsals, advertising, or booking a theatre. A licensing fee must be paid whether the title(s) is presented for charity or gain and whether or not admission is charged. Professional/Stock licensing fees are quoted upon application to Concord Theatricals Corp.

This work is published by Samuel French, an imprint of Concord Theatricals Corp.

No one shall make any changes in this title(s) for the purpose of production. No part of this book may be reproduced, stored in a retrieval system, scanned, uploaded, or transmitted in any form, by any means, now known or yet to be invented, including mechanical, electronic, digital, photocopying, recording, videotaping, or otherwise, without the prior written permission of the publisher. No one shall share this title(s), or any part of this title(s), through any social media or file hosting websites.

For all inquiries regarding motion picture, television, online/digital and other media rights, please contact Concord Theatricals Corp.

MUSIC AND THIRD PARTY MATERIALS USE NOTE

Licensees are solely responsible for obtaining formal written permission from copyright owners to use copyrighted music and/or other copyrighted third-party materials (e.g., artworks, logos) in the performance of this play and are strongly cautioned to do so. If no such permission is obtained by the licensee, then the licensee must use only original music and materials that the licensee owns and controls. Licensees are solely responsible and liable for clearances of all third-party copyrighted materials, including without limitation music, and shall indemnify the copyright owners of the play(s) and their licensing agent, Concord Theatricals Corp., against any costs, expenses, losses and liabilities arising from the use of such copyrighted third-party materials by licensees. For music, please contact the appropriate music licensing authority in your territory for the rights to any incidental music.

IMPORTANT BILLING AND CREDIT REQUIREMENTS

If you have obtained performance rights to this title, please refer to your licensing agreement for important billing and credit requirements.

ABOUT THESPIAN PLAYWORKS

Thespian Playworks is a writing contest and script-development program for high school students, sponsored by the Educational Theatre Association and run by the staff of *Dramatics* magazine. Each year, up to four finalists are invited to the International Thespian Festival, where the students work with a professional director, a dramaturg, and a volunteer cast of actors to put their short plays on their feet before a live audience.

Launched in 1994 as a tribute to longtime International Thespian Society executive Doug Finney, the program aims to nurture young playwrights, and over Playworks' history, many participants have gone on to college majors and careers in theatre, writing, and related fields. Whatever the eventual future of the writers or their scripts, Playworks is an exhilarating experience in a creative discipline seldom taught in schools or celebrated in the wider culture.

The call for entries goes out each fall, with submission deadlines in mid-winter. *Dramatics* receives scores of scripts from high school thespians all over the U.S., Canada, and as far away as the United Arab Emirates. Each play is reviewed at least twice, as teams of readers (including *Dramatics* staff and other professional critics and theatre artists) narrow down the entries: first to a dozen semifinalists, then to the final four. Each semifinalist receives a personal letter with feedback on his or her script.

For more on Thespian Playworks, please visit www.edta.org/playworks.

CONTENTS

Placebo 7
Stratocumulus 29
Derailed. 49
Umtya (The String) 65

PLACEBO

Tan'yeasia Brewster

PLACEBO, by Tan'yeasia Brewster of Troupe 8117 at Nuview Bridge Early College High School in Nuevo, California, was presented in a staged reading as part of the Thespian Playworks program at the 2018 International Thespian Festival on June 30, 2018. The production was directed by Michael Daehn, with dramaturgy by Stephen Gregg. The stage manager was Gage Pipkin. The cast was as follows:

AMAYA	Marisa Turner
JESSIE	Sam Barrett
KIM	Katie Howard
DEVAN	Kyle Swearingen
ISABEL	Meghan van Dobben
LUCAS	Mark Daniel
DOCTOR / MOM	Emma Miller
MS. MONROE	Amelia Gorman

CHARACTERS

AMAYA – High school senior. Her amygdala has been damaged since she was a small child, which has lead her to be without emotions and to be oblivious to some social cues. Amaya is striving to feel something, which is why she ingests yellow paint. In the first half of the play it should seem like she has no emotions, but frustration is clearly right below the surface. She develops a crush on Jessie.

JESSIE – High school senior, teaching Amaya an accelerated art course. Jessie is very happy, should smile a lot. She wants to go to art school but is afraid of actually pursuing it. She should never appear to be talking down to Amaya, or be hesitant to speak her mind. She develops a crush on Amaya.

KIM – Amaya's mom and Devan's wife. The type of person who believes ignorance is bliss, she is in denial that Amaya needs help. She talks down to Amaya, and while she does love her, more often than not she is frustrated with how her daughter is.

DEVAN – Amaya's dad and Kim's husband. He loves Amaya very much but hasn't put much effort into helping her.

ISABEL – Amaya's closest friend. While Isabel is mean and selfish, she shouldn't come off as just a stereotypical mean girl. Throughout the flashbacks she should venture from bully into someone for whom you can empathize.

LUCAS – Amaya's friend. Lucas isn't mean to Amaya, he's just honest.

MR. MONROE / ART GALLERY GUY – One male actor should play both. Monroe is Amaya's school counselor. He's professional and shouldn't show a bias toward Amaya. As Art Gallery Guy, he's the one who Jessie goes off to talk to.

DOCTOR / MOM – One female actor should play both. Doctor is Amaya's doctor. Mom is Isabel's mother in the first flashback.

PROP LIST

Canvas: Audience does not see the front of the canvas, only the back.
Watch: An average plastic watch.
Yellow paint and paintbrush: Paint could be water and food coloring, something edible.
Sketchbook: Audience does not see what's inside.

(This opening segment is three groups happening at once:)
(Group 1: **ISABEL** *and* **LUCAS.***)*
(Group 2: **KIM, DEVAN,** *and* **MR. MONROE.***)*
(Group 3: **DOCTOR.***)*
*(***AMAYA** *is speaking to the audience.)*

AMAYA. Yesterday, I stepped in front of a moving bus.
KIM. What were you thinking?
ISABEL. You just love the attention, don't you?
DEVAN. Amaya, I can't keep missing work because of this.
AMAYA. I didn't do it on purpose.
MR. MONROE. I believe this might be a cry for help.
LUCAS. Maybe you should talk to a professional.
AMAYA. I just forgot to look both ways.
DOCTOR. It's another symptom for her –
KIM. Don't say it.
AMAYA. Disease, deficit, disorder.
MR. MONROE. On campus, she's become a walking liability.
KIM. Amaya, why do you have to be so difficult?
MR. MONROE. Students say she looked the bus driver directly in the eye before she walked off the curb.
DEVAN. Is that true, Amaya? You know you can talk to us. We were in high school too once, we probably know how you feel.
AMAYA. Feel. F-e-e-l, to experience an emotion or sensation.
DEVAN. We should've just listened to the doctors.
DOCTOR. Your daughter is a health phenomenon.
AMAYA. As a child, I used to play hide and seek with myself. I would hide in the cupboards, in closets, or under my

bed. I used to do it so often that my dad insisted we went to see a doctor.

KIM. This is so stupid. All children are different, so what if our daughter likes to be left alone?

DOCTOR. We ran a couple tests and discovered some damage.

DEVAN. Damage?

DOCTOR. The amygdala seems to not be functioning properly.
(Pointing to what would be a brain scan.) If you look right here –

AMAYA. People say I'm –

LUCAS. Broken.

ISABEL. Odd.

KIM. Fine! She is fine.

(**LUCAS** *and* **ISABEL** *exit.*)

DOCTOR. Maybe after therapy, and some pills –

KIM. Pills? You've got to be kidding me! Make up a fake illness so we pay for medication every month for the rest of her life. No.

(**DOCTOR** *leaves.*)

MR. MONROE. Yesterday she ate a handful of the soap in the girls' bathroom.

AMAYA. I wanted to know how it tasted.

MR. MONROE. During rock climbing in PE, she climbed to the top, unbuckled herself and then jumped.

AMAYA. How else was I supposed to get down?

MR. MONROE. The point of this meeting is that Amaya only really has her art credit left to complete and then she can graduate. The school has offered to send in someone to personally teach the lesson plan. It shouldn't take too long.

(**MR. MONROE** *exits.* **KIM** *and* **DEVAN** *exit after acknowledging* **AMAYA** *in some way.* **JESSIE** *enters.* **AMAYA** *sits in a new spot to show that time has passed and they're in a new space.*)

JESSIE. Only eight weeks. This should be really easy. You just have to complete four paintings and a couple quizzes.

AMAYA. Aren't you a bit young to be a teacher?

JESSIE. I'm a senior. We go to, or used to go to the same high school. My name's Jessie. Mr. Monroe is letting me teach you and in return I get community service and it'll go on my college applications.

AMAYA. Are you applying for art school or something?

JESSIE. What? No, I couldn't. While I would love to paint for a living, I don't want to be another starving artist. I'm going to major in general biology instead. What about you?

AMAYA. What about me?

JESSIE. What are you going to do after you graduate?

(**AMAYA** *doesn't know.*)

It's okay if you don't know yet. Plenty of people don't.

AMAYA. It's just no one's really ever asked me that before.

JESSIE. Really? Not even your parents? Because mine are constantly bugging me about what practical, sustainable career I'm going to pursue.

AMAYA. My parents are too busy.

JESSIE. Oh, I guess you'll have to get all your nagging from me then.

(*Beat.*)

So for the first project, you'll paint something abstract. I brought you a canvas and a bunch of different colors of paint. I figured we could just knock out the first project now.

(**JESSIE** *hands* **AMAYA** *the blank canvas and digs in her bag for paint.*)

AMAYA. I've never actually painted before. I don't know what I would even...

JESSIE. It's okay, I'll guide you through it. So abstract painting isn't about being technical or exact, it's basically just using a bunch of colors on a canvas to describe how you feel.

AMAYA. How I feel?

JESSIE. Yeah, like using blue for sadness, red for anger, green for ambition, the list goes on and on. Every color has some sort of emotion attached to it.

AMAYA. *(Staring down at her canvas with a blank expression.)* Well then, here you go. My canvas is already done.

> *(Gives it to* **JESSIE.***)*

JESSIE. But it's blank?

> *(***AMAYA** *doesn't say anything.* **JESSIE** *stares at her for a moment.)*

Would you like to see an example maybe? Here's an abstract painting I finished the other day. Look at it and tell me what you feel.

AMAYA. It's very yellow.

JESSIE. Yellow makes me feel happy. I think yellow could make anyone feel happy, just like smiling even when you're upset. It forces you to feel better regardless.

AMAYA. But...it's just a color.

> *(***AMAYA** *is confused, not defensive.)*

JESSIE. Yeah, but it represents more. This yellow paint is also sunshine, optimism, energy and joy.

AMAYA. Does everyone feel yellow?

JESSIE. No, not everyone. I think that's why I like art so much, because for just a moment they can look at a painting – I mean really look at a painting, and for one moment they're viewing another world and in this world I can use as much yellow as I'd like.

> *(***AMAYA** *is confused, staring at this paint as if it's magical.)*

Y'know it's rumored that Van Gogh used to eat yellow paint so he could feel happy.

AMAYA. Did it work?

> *(***JESSIE** *exits.* **AMAYA** *walks forward toward the audience as if she's looking in a mirror.*

She dips the paintbrush in yellow paint and paints a stripe on her tongue. She then does a big, obnoxious smile. It doesn't reach her eyes; she's again just trying Jessie's advice. A moment passes. **JESSIE** *enters, perhaps on the opposite side from before to show that time has passed.)*

JESSIE. Morning! I felt like the coffee shop is better than just sitting at my kitchen table. So did you finish assignment number two, the representational painting? I'm hoping a week was enough time.

AMAYA. Yeah, I finished it.

JESSIE. You didn't leave it blank like the abstract one did you?

AMAYA. You said that assignment was about how you feel. Mine showed that.

JESSIE. Fair enough. But this painting is literal. It should be like looking at a photograph of your life. So what did you paint?

(**AMAYA** *hands* **JESSIE** *a canvas.* **JESSIE** *lifts the canvas up, covering her face, detaching from the scene.* **KIM, ISABEL,** *and* **MOM** *enter.)*

AMAYA. When I was nine, my mom got a new camera. So she took me to the park to take pictures for her blog.

KIM. I'm gonna take photos of these flowers first, and then I'll take some of you, so don't get dirty. But don't just stand there. Go make friends! Look isn't that girl in your class? Go say hi! Go!

(**AMAYA** *trudges over to* **ISABEL.**)

ISABEL. What are *you* doing here?

AMAYA. My mom says I need to make friends.

ISABEL. I already have friends. Lots and lots of friends.

AMAYA. Oh, well, I could be another friend.

ISABEL. You know everyone says you're weird. You don't laugh or smile or do anything.

AMAYA. My dad says there's nothing wrong with being weird. Do you want to play tag?

ISABEL. Fine. Tag, you're it.

(**ISABEL** *pokes* **AMAYA**.)

AMAYA. Should I start counting?

(**ISABEL** *doesn't say anything, so* **AMAYA** *closes her eyes and counts anyway.*)

One, two, three –

ISABEL. (*Pokes* **AMAYA** *quite roughly.*) Tag, you're it.

AMAYA. I know, I didn't finish counting. One, two, three –

ISABEL. (*Pokes her harder.*) Tag, you're it.

AMAYA. One, two –

ISABEL. (*Pokes her again.*) Do you know how to play tag?

AMAYA. One, two, three –

ISABEL. (*Pokes her again.*) I said, "Tag you're it!"

AMAYA. Stop it.

ISABEL. (*Pokes her again.*) Why? You probably don't even feel anything.

(*Pokes her again.*)

You're just like a doll.

(**AMAYA** *pushes* **ISABEL**. *She falls to the ground and cries.* **MOM** *and* **KIM** *rush over.*)

MOM. Isabel!

ISABEL. She pushed me!

KIM. Oh! I am so sorry!

MOM. It's fine. I totally understand, I have a niece who's slow too.

KIM. Slow? Um, excuse me? My daughter is just like yours, there's nothing wrong with her!

(**MOM** *and* **ISABEL** *exit.*)

Amaya! Look at me. Am I happy?

AMAYA. Yes.

KIM. Amaya, we went over this. Look at my face, am I happy?

AMAYA. *(To audience.)* This stuff is supposed to come naturally but there might as well be a cement slab up in the middle of my mind.

KIM. Amaya, pay attention. What's this one.

AMAYA. Smile, happy.

KIM. Good.

AMAYA. Brows, confused.

KIM. Yes.

AMAYA. Frown, sad.

KIM. Yes, good, good, good. See I told you.

DEVAN. Kim, just because she remembers the cards doesn't mean she actually understands. Flashcards aren't a substitute to actually seeing a doctor.

(**DEVAN** *picks up another card.*)

Amaya, what about this one.

AMAYA. The eyebrows are down…and it's a frown.

KIM. Yes so what is it?

AMAYA. Sad?

KIM. No.

AMAYA. Surprised.

KIM. No.

AMAYA. Disgust?

KIM. No! Amaya, we just went over this. You know what they are.

DEVAN. Don't yell at her. This one is fear. Do you know what that is?

AMAYA. No.

DEVAN. Do you know what any of these are?

AMAYA. Frown, sad. Smile, happy.

DEVAN. But what does that mean, sweetie?

(**AMAYA** *doesn't know.*)

DEVAN. Kim, this is why I said we need to see a doctor.

KIM. We don't need a doctor. They don't know her better than I do.

Amaya, remember the other cards? Today I feel. Today what do you feel.

(**AMAYA** *touches her face.*)

DEVAN. Kim, you're overwhelming her.

KIM. I am not. Amaya look at the cards which do you feel?

(**AMAYA** *continues to touch her face.*)

DEVAN. You know it's not so bad if she needs professional help. Our daughter is wonderful, whether she understands the cards or not.

KIM. Amaya stop touching your face and pick a card! Amaya, pick a card. How do you feel.

AMAYA. I don't frown or smile and my eyebrows don't furrow. So, nothing.

DEVAN. And that's okay, Amaya. Kim, just stop with the cards.

KIM. It's not okay. What about when you play with your toys Amaya, or talk to kids at school. Doesn't that make you feel happy?

AMAYA. No.

KIM. Then what does?

(**AMAYA** *doesn't know.* **KIM** *uses her hand and forces* **AMAYA***'s mouth up into a smile. A small moment passes before* **KIM** *leaves the stage.* **JESSIE** *puts the painting down.*)

JESSIE. You know they're wrong, right? You're not weird, and you're not a doll. Anyone who has anything negative to say about you, just feels so bad about their own sad lives that they try to make you feel bad too.

(*Beat.*)

And for what it's worth, I think you're pretty cool.

(**JESSIE** *exits.* **AMAYA** *walks forward toward the audience as if she's looking in a mirror. She dips the paintbrush in yellow paint and paints a stripe on her tongue.*)

AMAYA. Pretty cool.

(**AMAYA** *does the tiniest hint of a smile, like a young girl developing a crush. A small moment passes before* **AMAYA** *goes to the table and grabs a notebook and begins flipping through it.* **JESSIE** *enters; it's a new day and this meeting is more casual.*)

Are all these people you drew, your friends and family or something?

JESSIE. Yeah…uh give it back.

AMAYA. Is that me?

JESSIE. Maybe? Would you be weirded out if it was? Because I wasn't planning on drawing you or anything. I just came home and I was thinking about you and, uh that sounds weird.

(*Beat.*)

But like you do this thing where you don't really smile but your eyes like, y'know. I'm just going to be quiet.

AMAYA. My eyes what?

JESSIE. I don't know… Sometimes they just give it all away. You say you've never been happy but sometimes your eyes get big and it's like you smile with your eyes.

AMAYA. It's probably from all that paint.

JESSIE. What?

AMAYA. Nothing. So what kind of art would this be?

JESSIE. This is a continuous line charcoal sketch. Meaning every line is connected, because I think it not only shows the impact people have had on your life but the impact you have on others. And charcoal is really neat because you have to be precise with it because one part could turn into a smudge if you're too hard but if you're too light you'll barely see it, like with your eyes. I filled one in so it's dark but left the other one light it shows the parallel between nothing and everything. I think it's really beautiful.

> (*A small moment between* **JESSIE** *and* **AMAYA**. **JESSIE** *likes* **AMAYA**, *and* **AMAYA** *likes* **JESSIE**. **AMAYA** *should have a hint of a smile on her face.*)

It sucks that you're already halfway done with the course, but with your art and quizzes Mr. Monroe agrees that you'll finish with an A.

> (**AMAYA** *just shrugs in response.*)

So, what did you paint this week?

> (**AMAYA** *hands* **JESSIE** *the canvas.* **JESSIE** *looks at it, covering her face to detach from the scene.*)

AMAYA. It's an impressionist piece, from a time when I was about twelve.

> (**ISABEL** *enters.* **AMAYA** *steps forward.*)

A movie?

ISABEL. Yes, a movie. You know every time I come over all we do is our homework and then spend the rest of the day staring at the freaking walls. Plus, Lucas wants to watch a movie.

AMAYA. But, we've never hung out with Lucas before.

ISABEL. So? He wanted to come over, also he has a pretty nice watch on his wrist that can be ours...if you take it.

AMAYA. Steal it? Why do I have to do that?

ISABEL. Because I said so. It doesn't hurt to have a little bit of fun, Amaya. Now shut up, Lucas is coming back.

LUCAS. Your house is really nice, Amaya. And thank you for inviting me over. I know everyone says you're a bit off but I don't think so.

ISABEL. How nice. Now shut up so I can start the movie.

(*The three of them sit facing the audience at what would be the "movie."* **LUCAS** *is laughing and completely engrossed in it.* **ISABEL** *is also fascinated, laughing occasionally, while* **AMAYA** *sits there watching their reactions instead of the actual movie.* **ISABEL** *turns to* **AMAYA** *and shoots her a look, which* **AMAYA** *ignores.*)

Now!

LUCAS. What?

ISABEL. I said, Wow. Anakin is really cute.

LUCAS. I mean he's not bad-looking. Me and Tommy used to watch this movie all the time, before he…got sick. This movie used to always make him feel better…or at least I thought it did. Now I just watch it alone. And I know he's been gone for a while and I shouldn't be sad because no one wants to hang out with the sad kid. Which really sucks because it gets lonely, I always –

(**ISABEL** *shoots* **AMAYA** *another look.* **AMAYA** *takes the watch out of* **LUCAS'** *pocket but accidentally drops it on the floor.*)

What are you doing?

(**ISABEL** *and* **LUCAS** *both lean down to grab the watch.* **ISABEL** *takes it first.*)

Isabel, give that back!

ISABEL. Amaya, catch.

(**AMAYA** *catches it.*)

LUCAS. Amaya, please give it back.

(**AMAYA** *is frozen.* **LUCAS** *goes to snatch it from her, but it falls. He then goes to reach for it, but* **AMAYA** *steps on it before he can.*)

ISABEL. *(Laughing.)* Oh my gosh, how am I going to wear it now?

LUCAS. Is that why you guys invited me over? To steal my watch?

ISABEL. It's a fancy watch.

LUCAS. It was made out of plastic! We're in the seventh grade why would I own an expensive watch?!

ISABEL. But you said it was valuable?

LUCAS. Because this is the last thing that I have of my best friend. And now you broke it! I always knew that Isabel was mean, so I didn't get why you hung out with her Amaya. But now I get it! You're her little doll, because you can't think for yourself!

(**LUCAS** *runs offstage.* **DEVAN** *enters.* **AMAYA** *brings her hands toward her eyes.*)

DEVAN. Who is that boy and why is he crying?

ISABEL. I don't know some people are just really sensitive.

DEVAN. Oh, hi Isabel. I think I saw your mom outside.

(**ISABEL** *exits.*)

Amaya, what are you doing?

AMAYA. Eye irritation leads to tears.

DEVAN. Okay? Why are you trying to cry?

(**AMAYA** *doesn't answer.*)

Sometimes crying can be therapeutic. But let it come naturally, Maya. Stop it.

(**DEVAN** *moves* **AMAYA**'s *hands from her eyes.*)

AMAYA. Dolls can't cry, Dad.

DEVAN. You're not a doll, Amaya. You're a lot of things but that's not one of them.

AMAYA. Then what am I?

DEVAN. You're my little girl. My sweet little blessing. I know sometimes things can get hard, Maya. And I admire your strength, and courage, and –

(**AMAYA** *presses her fingers to her eyes.*)

No!

AMAYA. Ow.

DEVAN. You're so silly. So, so silly. My silly girl.

> *(Laughing then crying, he holds **AMAYA** to his chest for a moment. Then he exits.)*

JESSIE. Are you still close with your dad?

AMAYA. He started working long hours. So, I don't see him much.

JESSIE. And how does that make you feel?

AMAYA. Nothing. It makes me feel nothing.

JESSIE. What are you so afraid of, Amaya? I can see it on your face and in your art that you want more but it's like you're shutting the door and not giving yourself a chance.

AMAYA. Don't say it like I've never tried.

JESSIE. Have you?

AMAYA. Have you? You know what makes you happy but you refuse to pursue it because "what-ifs" scare you.

JESSIE. No it doesn't. I just –

AMAYA. I was on my laptop last night and I found this art exhibition for next week it's being hosted by the head of the art department at SYU. If we go maybe you could talk to him.

JESSIE. SYU? The college of my dreams, SYU? I don't know, Amaya. Those showcases aren't free.

AMAYA. I already bought the tickets.

JESSIE. You did? Amaya, I don't think I – wait, tickets for me and you, the two of us?

AMAYA. Yeah, think of it as a field trip.

JESSIE. Field trip, right.

> *(**JESSIE** exits. **AMAYA** walks forward toward the audience as if she's looking in a mirror. She dips the paintbrush in yellow paint and paints a stripe on her tongue. She smiles, slightly bigger than the one before. All cast members except **KIM** and **DEVAN** enter.)*

I've never actually been to an art show before.

AMAYA. Me neither.

JESSIE. You look great.

AMAYA. You too.

JESSIE. Oh gosh, look he's finally alone. I should go talk to him, right?

AMAYA. Yes, go. I'll be right here, looking at the art.

JESSIE. Okay, wish me luck.

> (**JESSIE** *goes to talk to* **ART GALLERY GUY**. **AMAYA** *looks at what would be art. There is a canvas on the ground; she reaches down to touch it and everyone onstage freezes for a moment before transitioning into a new scene.* **LUCAS** *and* **ISABEL** *walk pass* **AMAYA**.)

AMAYA. *(To audience.)* After middle school, Lucas, Isabel and I became inseparable. But lately it's been more them than us.

LUCAS. Don't come over.

AMAYA. Why not? We always hang out after school.

ISABEL. Look, Amaya. Lucas and I have been talking and we think maybe we shouldn't hang out together anymore.

AMAYA. Is it something that I did?

ISABEL. It's not always about you, Amaya. You know in the eight years that we've been *friends* we haven't learned anything about each other. You never talk to me about what's wrong with you and you can barely empathize enough to hold a proper conversation.

AMAYA. *(To audience.)* I used to wonder what it would feel like to be trapped in quicksand. To slowly sink farther and farther into the sand, and no matter how hard you tried still you were stuck.

ISABEL. I'm talking to you, Amaya!

AMAYA. *(To audience.)* Quicksand isn't deep enough for you to drown in it. But if you stay in it too long, the pressure can cut off your circulation. Leaving you numb.

LUCAS. Amaya, maybe you should talk to someone. Get some help.

AMAYA. Help?

> (**LUCAS** and **ISABEL** start to walk away.)

Wait!

JESSIE. What are you so afraid of?

ISABEL. You're just like a doll.

KIM. Why do you have to be so difficult?

DEVAN. My silly, silly girl.

LUCAS. Whatever you're looking for, you're not gonna find it in us.

> (**LUCAS** and **ISABEL** exit.)

AMAYA. What am I looking for?

JESSIE. Watch out for the bus!

> (**AMAYA** takes a step forward, then a quick jolt backward and clutches her stomach. Back to present time.)

Amaya! Guess what he invited me down for an interview next week! I can't believe – are you okay?

AMAYA. Everything's spinning

> (**AMAYA** falls backward. **KIM** and **DEVAN** enter, lay her into a chair/bench, now in **DOCTOR**'s office. **JESSIE** exits.)

DOCTOR. It's poisoning.

KIM. What do you mean? Like food poisoning?

DOCTOR. No, it looks like your daughter has been ingesting paint. We'll have to keep her for a while to flush it all out.

> (**DOCTOR** exits.)

KIM. Paint? Why would you eat paint, Amaya?!

AMAYA. I don't know.

DEVAN. Maya, please just talk to us. What's been going on?

AMAYA. Nothing. Nothing has been going on.

KIM. Really? You expect us to believe you're in the hospital for nothing.

AMAYA. *(Finally voicing her frustration.)* That's exactly why! Because I am on a constant loop of nothing. I am stuck in nothing, feeling nothing, doing nothing.

(Beat.)

And you both are doing nothing about it!

KIM. What are we supposed to do, Amaya?! I don't have all the answers, but I have been trying to raise you the best that I can. Give you unlimited opportunities and teach you that there is nothing wrong with you.

AMAYA. Not acknowledging the problem doesn't make it go away. I think I'd like to see a therapist.

KIM. Therapist? Maya, I'm not letting them put you on medication.

AMAYA. I just want to talk to someone, a professional who can help me sort through all of this.

KIM. Amaya –

DEVAN. I think that's a good idea. Your mom and I need to realize that this is beyond us. We've always wanted the best for you, and for the last seventeen years the best we've given you hasn't been enough. We'll go talk to the doctor and see if she recommends anyone.

*(**DEVAN** and a reluctant **KIM** exit. **JESSIE** enters.)*

JESSIE. Are you okay? I stopped by last night but your mom told me to come today instead.

AMAYA. Jessie! I finished the last painting!

JESSIE. What? Amaya, who cares about the painting. I was so worried –

*(**AMAYA** hands **JESSIE** a canvas.)*

The last painting was supposed to be a self-portrait. So why did you draw me?

AMAYA. Living with my condition has been hard. Most people think I'm weird, or broken, but you don't. You've been the only person to look at me and see more than I ever did. And with your art you've brought me into your world, your very yellow world.

JESSIE. The paint? Amaya, I never meant for you to –

AMAYA. All my life, I have been looking for more – looking to feel something, and the way you smiled when we first met showed me that you had it. So I thought it was in the paint. And I thought it was working but even without it, my heart beats fast, my skin gets hot, and I smile.

JESSIE. Oh.

AMAYA. So I used bright colors. I made your irises and mouth yellow because you're always laughing. But your pupils are blue from dreams you think you'll miss out on. Your hands are red from the passion of your art. The base of your skin is green because you remind me of nature, and I used hints of orange to highlight it all because you're like fire and my hands are cold.

JESSIE. Amaya –

AMAYA. And you've made me feel... I feel, um my, when I. Dammit, I don't know what it is. But you make me, uh. I feel.

> (**AMAYA** *gives up on words. They stare at each other.* **JESSIE** *waits, even slightly leans in until* **AMAYA** *takes a step forward and they kiss.*)

JESSIE. I like you too.

> (**AMAYA** *smiles.*)

End of Play

STRATOCUMULUS

Sofia Bottinelli

STRATOCUMULUS, by Sofia Bottinelli of Troupe 5869 at Denver School of the Arts, was presented in a staged reading as part of the Thespian Playworks program at the 2018 International Thespian Festival on June 30, 2018. The production was directed by Carolyn Cork Greer, with dramaturgy by Nicholas C. Pappas. The stage manager was Zachary Holzberg. The cast was as follows:

PIPER	Julissa Lopez
REESE	Jack O'Donoghue

CHARACTERS

PIPER – Standoffish. She is highly closed off and tends to guard her true feelings. She has gone through a lot in her short years and doesn't know how to handle her emotions or those of others. Sarcasm is her defense mechanism: if one can't tell if she is being sarcastic or not, then odds are she probably is. Sixteen years old.

REESE – Bright. It seems he is always happy, and he never fails to lighten the mood. Laughter is his defense mechanism, but he says exactly what he thinks. He rarely notices the good he brings out in others and constantly underestimates himself. Sixteen years old.

SETTING

The shed of a nondescript high school. Late afternoon.

AUTHOR'S NOTE

Shorter dialogue should be fast-paced to keep the action moving. Be careful of adding unnecessary beats. Ellipses [...] buy time for thinking.

(**PIPER** *sits on the roof of an old shed that is covered in spray paint. The door to the shed is slightly ajar, revealing lacrosse sticks and other aging sporting equipment. The front of the shed reads "Go Griffins!"* **PIPER** *is partially covered by the shadow of the high school behind her, and the afternoon is holding its breath as evening begins to set in.*)

REESE. *(Shouting from the ground.)* Hey! It's Piper right?

(**PIPER** *looks down but does not respond.*)

Um, would you mind coming down from the roof for a minute?

(*No response.* **REESE** *appears increasingly uncomfortable.*)

Look, I'm supposed to interview you for the new student profile section in the school paper. Would you mind coming down? It will only take a second, I promise.

(*Long pause.*)

PIPER. I'm not getting down.

REESE. Why not? Isn't your favorite song "Low" by Flo Rida? Shouldn't getting down sort of be your thing?

PIPER. I'm sorry, what did you just say to me?

REESE. Uh…you know. *(Hesitantly.)* Apple bottom jeans and boots with the fur…

(*He awkwardly dances for a couple of beats.*)

(*Several beats pass.*)

Oh, come on, you must have something to say now!

PIPER. Um…do you have any soap?

REESE. What?

PIPER. I think I need to wash out my eyes. And my ears.

REESE. But Facebook said that was your favorite song!

PIPER. Yeah, the last time I updated that thing I was twelve years...wait you were on my Facebook! Dude, you need to take a few steps back, so you aren't in violation of the restraining order I'm about to get on you.

REESE. I'm sorry! It was just...research. Yeah, research.

PIPER. Research for what?

REESE. I told you! I'm supposed to interview you for the... new student section of the newspaper.

PIPER. No thanks.

REESE. If I don't do it someone else will. The...the principal specifically asked for you.

PIPER. The principal doesn't even know who I am.

REESE. I don't know what to tell you. We are on a deadline though so...

PIPER. Well, it looks like it's going to rain, so you should probably find me another time. You don't want to get caught in a storm up here.

REESE. It's not going to rain.

PIPER. And you know that because you're some sort of high school meteorologist or...

REESE. I just know.

PIPER. You know what? Fine. Whatever. You only have two minutes though, and I reserve the right to push you off whenever I feel like it.

REESE. Works for me!

(He finds footholds on the shed door but drops most of his books on the way up to the roof.)

(Continuing to struggle.) I'm good, I'm good! This is easier than it looks.

PIPER. You dropped stuff.

REESE. *(Awkwardly.)* Oh, I can just get it later. Um, hi... I'm Reese.

(He puts his hand out to shake.)

PIPER. *(Looking at his outstretched hand.)* I know.
>   *(Beat.)*

You sit behind me in biology.
REESE. *(Dropping his hand.)* Right. Sorry.
PIPER. Why?
REESE. Why what?
PIPER. Why are you sorry?
REESE. I guess it's just a thing people say.
PIPER. I think people say it too much. It doesn't have much meaning anymore.
REESE. Right. Sorry.
>   *(**PIPER** gives him a pointed look.)*

(Flustered.) Oh. Sorry! ...Crap. You're right.
PIPER. Yeah, I know.
>   *(**REESE** laughs.)*

Ninety seconds remaining.
REESE. Okay, well, then is it all right if I ask you some questions now?
PIPER. Can we skip that part?
REESE. That's the whole part though.
PIPER. It was worth a try. Fine. Eighty seconds.
REESE. Awesome! Okay, let's see here...
>   *(**REESE** pulls a notepad and pencil from his biggest bag.)*

What keeps you up at night?
PIPER. Oh, sure, let me just bare my soul to you.
REESE. It doesn't have to be a complete baring. So, tell me then.
PIPER. Well, there's this one cricket somewhere outside my house that's just always making that cricket sound, you know? So, I'm sitting there trying to fall asleep and –
REESE. You know what I mean.
PIPER. I answered the question.

REESE. Not the one I was asking.

PIPER. I don't have an answer.

REESE. That's not true. Everyone's got something.

PIPER. It doesn't matter if I do or don't now anyway. Time's up.

REESE. What? No, those terms aren't valid anymore.

PIPER. I let you ask me a question, and now your time is up. What could be more valid?

REESE. You didn't answer honestly, so everything else is null and void.

PIPER. That wasn't a term of our agreement.

REESE. It's my term. So, Piper, what keeps you up at night? I'm not leaving until you answer.

PIPER. You'll have to, because I'm not answering. I plead the fifth.

REESE. *(Laughing.)* Oh, come on! This isn't even a hard one!

PIPER. Five minutes ago, you'd never even said two words to me! Excuse me for not wanting to tell you my innermost thoughts.

REESE. Gotta start somewhere, right?

PIPER. Can we just not start at all?

REESE. You really don't like talking to people, do you?

    (Beat.)

Okay, let's start with something easier. Ah! All right. If you could ask Neil Armstrong any question, what would it be?

PIPER. Hmm…well, I guess I'd probably ask how he feels that Buzz got a whole action figure storyline in the *Toy Story* movies, and he wasn't even mentioned.

REESE. This won't work, if you keep avoiding everything.

PIPER. What's in it for me?

REESE. *(Rummaging in his pockets.)* You can have this Tootsie Pop.

PIPER. You think I'd take a bribe?

REESE. Will you?

PIPER. *(Taking it.)* Yes. I happen to like these.
REESE. I know...Facebook.
PIPER. Yeah, maybe stop doing that.
REESE. It was a joke, I promise!
PIPER. Not a very funny one.
REESE. It was worth a laugh though. I mean, come on.
PIPER. I only laugh when things are funny. My standards are high.
REESE. I will make you laugh.
PIPER. Doubtful.
REESE. Well, we'll just have to see about that, won't we?

> *(Beat.)*

So, Neil Armstrong?
PIPER. Right... I think I would ask Neil Armstrong if it still hurts to look at the sun from outer space.

> *(Sees **REESE** waiting for more.)*

I mean, obviously, if you stare at it from the surface of Earth, it feels like all that light is focused on you. That's way too much for one person to handle. So, if you do it for too long – even indirectly, like through a reflection in water or snow – you go blind. But there's so much darkness in space. All that light has somewhere to go, and the sun suddenly doesn't feel so close anymore. It's sort of like being up here, you know? You can see the craziness of everyone below you, but you're sort of removed from it, so it can't bother you. You're just a quiet observer. I think it's one of those things that no one actually knows, unless they see it for themselves.

> *(**PIPER** notices **REESE**'s impressed stare and immediately shifts back to her closed-off state.)*

Or maybe it hurts just as badly, and Neil Armstrong didn't even get a chance to look and see.
REESE. Damn.
PIPER. *(Embarrassed.)* Anything else?

REESE. I think I need a minute to take all that in.

>   (*Beat.*)

PIPER. Can I ask *you* a question?

REESE. Yeah, shoot!

PIPER. Why are they doing a new student profile in the last month of school?

REESE. (*Hesitantly.*) Um, I guess the editors didn't think of it until a few days ago.

PIPER. And they didn't just wait until the beginning of next year?

REESE. Yeah…well the editors are seniors, so I think they just wanted to be able to be a part of it.

PIPER. Then how come you're here, instead of one of them?

REESE. They had…you know…senior things.
(*Changing the subject.*) Um, I think I need to warm you up for the hard questions!

>   (**PIPER** *looks at him questioningly.*)

Speed round.

PIPER. Oh, dear god.

REESE. No, it'll be fun. I promise! Ready…set…what's your favorite animal?

PIPER. Owl.

>   (*Almost overlapping:*)

REESE. Apple or Android?

PIPER. Oh, Apple, all the way.

REESE. Tea or coffee?

PIPER. Tea.

REESE. Favorite season?

PIPER. Fall.

REESE. Oceans or mountains?

PIPER. I'm more of a lake kind of girl.

REESE. Do you have a bucket list?

PIPER. In my head.

REESE. Something that's on it?
PIPER. Traveling the world.
REESE. Favorite place you *have* traveled?
PIPER. Greece.
REESE. Favorite book?
PIPER. All of them.
REESE. Favorite color?
PIPER. Brown.
REESE. Fav– ...brown?
PIPER. *(Laughing.)* What? I like it! It means things will start growing soon!
REESE. Was that a laugh?!
PIPER. *(Abruptly ceasing laughter.)* No.
REESE. Oh, it totally was! Piper zero, Reese one.
(In gladiator voice.) Are you not entertained?
PIPER. *(Smiling.)* Definitely not.
(Beat.)
So, what's this big warm-up for?
REESE. Right! This is a good one. Here we go.
(Whispering.) What...pause for effect...would be your perfect photograph?
PIPER. *(Quickly turning away.)* I don't take pictures.
REESE. We live in the age of technology! Who doesn't take pictures?
PIPER. *(Sharply.)* I don't.
REESE. No wonder your Facebook has been devoid of life for the last four years. You don't have any pictures to put on it! Why not just take some now?
PIPER. Because I don't want to!
REESE. Why?
PIPER. I just don't, okay? I don't have to explain it to you.
REESE. It just doesn't make sense though. Everyone takes pictures!
PIPER. Well, I'm not everyone!

REESE. What does that even mean?

PIPER. It means that I don't have to answer to you, so you can either let it go or leave!

REESE. Just tell me! It's no big deal! I want to know.

PIPER. I'm serious. Stop now.

REESE. Hey, it's okay! I'll back off. I'm sorry for pushing.

PIPER. Stop pushing, and you can stay.

REESE. Wait, you were serious about making me leave?

PIPER. Yes, but I just said you could stay. As long as you don't keep asking me that question.

REESE. I'm only trying to get to know you better.

PIPER. Why? It's not like you're ever going to talk to me again after this.

REESE. What do you mean?

PIPER. It's one section of the newspaper.

REESE. So?

PIPER. There won't be a reason for you to come up here after this.

REESE. What if I like it up here?

PIPER. What?

REESE. You heard me.

PIPER. It's my place!

REESE. It can be our place.

PIPER. Our place? Dude, you don't even know me.

REESE. But I'd like to.

PIPER. You could just stalk my Facebook again.

REESE. I told you, that was research!

PIPER. Why do you even care so much?

REESE. I'm just trying to help!

PIPER. I don't need your help, okay? And you sit here asking me all these questions on some high horse, while you can't even answer the simple one I just asked. You act like you're all superior, like you're somehow better than everyone. Well, guess what? You're not.

REESE. I'm sorry, I just –

PIPER. *(Angry.)* You just what? You just want to get to know me better? You just want to interrogate me and not leave me alone? You just want me to bare my soul to you, so you can laugh about it later? You seem like someone who always gets what they want, and I'm not gonna try to stop you now, so here it is. I don't take pictures anymore, because when I was five, I was completely obsessed with an old Polaroid camera. I took pictures of everything, and I especially loved taking pictures of people holding hands – some sort of childhood fantasy of people being able to find happiness in others, I guess. Well, one day, I took a picture of my parents holding hands. I found it in my room a few months later and hung it on my bedroom wall. When my mom saw it, she ripped it down and started to cry. I came in and found her sobbing on the floor. The next day, my parents told me that they'd finalized their divorce. I didn't even know what that meant, but I knew that my mom packed up her stuff and left. I waited for a whole day for her at the front door with the picture. When she never came home, I started to think that maybe taking pictures of my parents when they were happy was the reason they weren't anymore, that I was the reason their marriage fell apart. It doesn't make much sense, but it did to me then. So, yeah, I don't take pictures anymore. Who knows what I'll ruin next.

REESE. If you know it doesn't make sense, how come it still bothers you?

PIPER. I don't know. I also have an irrational fear of moths, but knowing it's irrational doesn't mean I can just make it go away.

(Beat.)

So, now you've pulled out my life story and have everything you need to leave me alone. You can go now.

(Beat.)

Okay, either say whatever it is your face is making that expression for or get off my roof.

REESE. *(Quietly.)* I'm just thinking that that must have been hard.

PIPER. Yeah, well, luckily for me, I don't think about it most of the time, until pricks like you decide it makes for a fun story.

REESE. Well, if you want a fun story, how about the fact that sometimes when no one is around to see, I pour milk into my bowl before the cereal, because I like to hear the splashy sound the cereal will make.

PIPER. Go to hell.

    (Beat.)

I'm sorry. I've never talked about that to anyone.

REESE. Me neither.

    (Attempting to lighten the mood.) And look who's saying sorry now?

PIPER. I actually mean it though.

REESE. Well, in that case, I accept your apology. So, um, how are you doing now?

PIPER. What?

REESE. I mean with your parents. Are you close or –

PIPER. *(Sarcastic.)* Will this be showing up in that article you're writing?

REESE. *(Not getting the sarcasm.)* Of course not! This is completely off the record.

PIPER. Uh – I, well, I hadn't talked to my mom in a few years. Last I checked, she was in Idaho somewhere. She moves around a lot. When she first left, I called her all the time, but pretty soon she just stopped calling me back. And then when I was twelve, I found her on Facebook, and her profile picture was of two little girls that looked a lot like me – her new family, I guess. I stopped reaching out to her after that. Now, I live with my dad, but he practically lives at work, so most of the time, it's just me and an empty house. But –

REESE. What?

PIPER. She called me two weeks ago.

REESE. That's great! Right?

PIPER. I don't know. She left a twenty-seven-second voicemail, but I've been too scared to listen to it.

REESE. Why?

PIPER. I guess I'm scared she'll want to see me, and I won't know what to say to her, but I'm more scared that she *won't* want to, and it'll be like she's leaving me all over again. That's why I'm sitting up here, telling you right now. I'm putting it off.

(Beat.)

REESE. Do you want me to listen to it with you? I can just sit up here with you, while you play it.

PIPER. I don't think we've reached that stage in our relationship just yet.

REESE. I just really think you should listen to it.

PIPER. Why?

REESE. Because it's your mom.

(Beat.)

You see those clouds up there?

PIPER. The rain clouds?

REESE. Well, they're actually not. They're called stratocumulus clouds, and you can only tell what they are, because they're shaped like dark clumps with little bits of light streaming through.

PIPER. So?

REESE. Having some darkness doesn't make them any less beautiful.

(Beat.)

PIPER. That was such a line.

REESE. A good one though, right?

PIPER. I've heard worse.

REESE. I'm serious though. They're...

PIPER. Yeah.

(They look at each other. PIPER breaks away first.)

PIPER. *(Clearing her throat.)* So, what about you?

REESE. Huh?

PIPER. I mean, I know I'm the one being interviewed, but I don't really think it's fair that you know my life story, and I don't know anything about you.

REESE. Oh. Well, there's not much to tell.

PIPER. Oh, please. Everyone's got something, right?

REESE. I wouldn't even know where to begin.

PIPER. Well, let's start with this. What keeps you up at night?

REESE. Easy. Nothing. I sleep like a baby.

PIPER. No.

REESE. Huh?

PIPER. Everyone's got something. How about…your biggest fears?

REESE. Also easy. I don't have any.

PIPER. I told you. You think you're better than everyone.

REESE. I do not.

PIPER. Then tell me.

REESE. Okay! Okay. Uh, yeah, okay. Well, when my mom got early-onset Alzheimer's –

PIPER. *(Sympathetic.)* Your mom has Alzheimer's?

REESE. Um…yeah. She was officially diagnosed four years ago. And every time she asks me to help her find her keys, when they're in her hand, or calls me by my dad's name – all I can think about is how it's genetic, you know? She started displaying symptoms when she was forty. That's barely more than twice my age right now, which means I only have twenty-four good years left. And I'm scared for her, of course I am, but…I'm scared for me, too. By the time I graduate college, I could be displaying symptoms. And I looked it up, and there's this DNA test you can do to see if your parent passed the genetic mutation down to you, and maybe I don't have it, but if I do, it's impossible to know if I'm just a carrier or if I will actually get the disease. So, I would just be waiting my whole life for it all to start, but what kind of life would that even be? So, I'm just watching this wonderful person fade away, and all I can think about is me. And that, at any time, I could start forgetting my mom and my friends and...even this moment. It's pretty selfish, I know.

PIPER. I don't think it's selfish.

REESE. Thanks. *(Uncomfortable.)* So, that's me.

PIPER. I don't get it.

*(She looks at **REESE** in contemplation.)*

REESE. *(Clearly uncomfortable with the attention.)* What do you mean?

PIPER. I wasn't nice to you. This whole time, I've snapped at you. And yet, when I told you about my family problems, which are completely incomparable to yours, you listened –

REESE. They aren't incomparable! You said it, too. Everyone has something.

PIPER. Some worse than others.

REESE. The way I see it, it's all about perspective. Yeah, it sucks to see my mom like this right now, but it doesn't take away from all the memories we've already made. And it's silly to compare hardships. I mean, the other day, I was making this sandwich, and it was about to be so good, right? It had ham and cheddar and tomatoes on this amazing sourdough bread, and I'd put it all together, was about to pick it up, reached over to grab a paper towel, and knocked the whole plate onto the floor. It was sad, but at least I got to enjoy the making of the sandwich. It's all about living in the moment, you know?

PIPER. That was a crazy analogy, but yeah...I do know. And I think I'd like to know you.

REESE. Really?

PIPER. Yeah. You're sort of wise.

REESE. Like an owl?

PIPER. What?

REESE. Your favorite animal, right? Aren't owls supposed to be all wise and stuff?

PIPER. I mean, I guess. If you learned about animal behavior from *Winnie the Pooh*, that is.

REESE. I'll have you know that Albert Einstein became interested in physics through *Winnie the Pooh*.

PIPER. He did?

REESE. No.

PIPER. *(Overlapping.)* Hey!

REESE. *(Overlapping.)* You make it too easy.

>   *(Beat. He offers **PIPER** his phone.)*

Take a picture.

PIPER. What? Why?

REESE. Well, aside from the fact that your taste in rooftops suggests that you have an eye for the picturesque, I think maybe it would bring you closure.

PIPER. Why are you doing this?

REESE. I just think it's not really fair that you took something away from yourself that made you happy. And I think it's holding you back. And right now, you have a chance to change. You have a chance to be happy.

PIPER. Oh, so you know exactly what I feel?

REESE. Of course not! It's just…I see your notebook in biology. You have all the right answers, and yet you never raise your hand, you never initiate conversations with anyone…it's been a year, and you still eat lunch by yourself. I know that coming in as a new student your junior year is weird, but it doesn't have to be this hard. And we're about to be seniors, and everyone should have a good senior year, because that's sort of the whole point of high school…and…and I think your mom made you so afraid to mess up other people's lives that now it's messing up yours. And that's not fair to you.

PIPER. *(Beat.)* You're right.

REESE. I am?

PIPER. I think so… Hey.

REESE. What?

PIPER. I'm glad you invaded my place.

REESE. Me, too.

PIPER. So...what will this article be called, so I can look for it in the paper?

REESE. It'll probably just be called "Student Interview with Piper Warren" or something equally boring.

PIPER. Wait, but isn't it multiple students?

REESE. Oh...yeah...right. It is.

PIPER. But you just said –

REESE. *(Sheepish.)* I –

PIPER. You what?

REESE. Don't be mad.

PIPER. You *what*?

REESE. Well... *(Speaking very quickly.)* I keep seeing you sitting up here, and I've noticed that you don't really have any friends and I wanted to make sure you were okay but you don't really strike me as someone who would tell a stranger that and so I thought maybe if I had a good excuse you would open up and we could maybe be friends and then you wouldn't have to eat lunch alone anymore and I just saw your doodles in your notebook and you seem really cool and I didn't know how to start a conversation so I –

> (**PIPER** *picks up her phone and takes a picture of* **REESE**, *almost surprising herself.*)

Did you just –

PIPER. *(Quietly, but smiling.)* Yeah.

REESE. Wow. Can I see it?

PIPER. *(Almost back to her usual self.)* Maybe, if you check my Facebook again.

REESE. It was one time!

PIPER. Sure it was. So...I'll see you tomorrow?

REESE. Definitely.

> *(He starts climbing down, none too gracefully.)*

REESE. *(Loudly.)* See you then!

PIPER. By the way, I knew you were lying about the paper.

REESE. What? No way.

PIPER. I can't help that you suck at lying. I was just waiting to find out why you bothered.

>*(She watches **REESE** picking up his books.)*

REESE. Don't make me come back up there!

PIPER. Bye, Reese!

REESE. Hey.

PIPER. Yeah?

REESE. Listen to the voicemail! Rip off the Band-Aid.

PIPER. *(Warningly.)* Reese.

REESE. Okay, fine, I'm going.

>*(He begins to leave.)*

Seriously though –

>*(He turns back to see **PIPER** with her phone. He smiles and leaves, humming. **PIPER** picks up the Tootsie Pop and smiles. When she sets it down, her eyes land on her phone.)*

PIPER. *(Quietly).* Okay, Mom.

>*(She brings the phone to her ear as the lights slowly fade.)*

End of Play

DERAILED

Jared Goudsmit

DERAILED, by Jared Goudsmit of Troupe 748 at Kirkwood High School in Kirkwood, Missouri, was presented in a staged reading as part of the Thespian Playworks program at the 2018 International Thespian Festival on June 30, 2018. The production was directed by William Myatt, with dramaturgy by Mark D. Kaufmann. The stage manager was Maxwell Plata. The cast was as follows:

THE NEFARIOUS BANDIT............................Daniel Tomalin
MISS MARIBEL..Molly Davis
THE DEPUTY ....Korben Smart

DERAILED was originally produced in the Blank Theatre Young Playwrights Festival in Los Angeles on May 31, 2018. The production was directed by Asaad Kelada, with dramaturgy by Robert L. Freedman. The stage manager was Marcedes Clanton. The cast was as follows:

THE NEFARIOUS BANDIT................................ Max Adler
MISS MARIBEL..................................... Jerrika Hinton
THE DEPUTY .... Jeff Torres

DERAILED was performed at SW1X at Kirkwood High School in Kirkwood, Missouri on November 9, 2017. The production was directed by Kristi Gunther. The stage manager was Alexis Terry. The cast was as follows:

THE NEFARIOUS BANDIT............................... Mark Perry
MISS MARIBEL......................................Natalie Scherr
THE DEPUTY ....Jamal Williams

CHARACTERS

THE NEFARIOUS BANDIT – Male. At first glance a traditional Wild West villain. In reality a lot less malicious and much more anxious.

MISS MARIBEL – Female. The woman tied to the railroad tracks. Pretty frustrated with the whole ordeal, as one might imagine.

THE DEPUTY – Male. A stereotypically bold, righteous hero.

SETTING

A western desert with a single set of railroad tracks running through what is otherwise a totally empty space.

(A distant train whistle sounds. **THE NEFARIOUS BANDIT**, *dressed in the garb of a feared outlaw, is trying to work out the final knot required to fully tie* **MISS MARIBEL**, *dressed as an 1800s schoolteacher, to the tracks. He wipes the sweat from his greasy handlebar mustache as he fumbles around with the ropes. Occasionally he gives up on his partially completed knot, pulling out his dagger and sawing his work away in frustration.* **MARIBEL** *is exasperated, not even bothering to struggle anymore. She glares at him. This goes on in silence for quite some time. The* **BANDIT**, *sensing hostility, looks away from the ropes for a moment.)*

BANDIT. It's really nothing personal. I want you to know that.

>*(Silence.)*

MARIBEL. Well, that makes me feel much better.

>*(More silence. The* **BANDIT**, *feeling awkward, goes back to tying the ropes. Beat.)*

BANDIT. So –

MARIBEL. If it isn't personal, then why are you tying…specifically…me to these tracks? Why – What is your…your motive? What do you gain from this?

BANDIT. Honestly? It's really just a…reputation thing. Look, the whole desperado business is huge here. Okay? The number of Western outlaws, and Western outlaw wannabes, is just…it's constantly just…skyrocketing. So, yes, as much as I'd like to do my own thing, be a lone wolf…all that. As much as I want to do that, it's just not where the money's at.

MARIBEL. *(Wrapping her head around things, incredulous.)* So, you're tying me to railroad tracks, to get me run over by an ironclad...steam locomotive, and it isn't even because of something I did?

BANDIT. Nope, sorry. Just trying to build my notoriety up.

MARIBEL. You know, if you're trying to intimidate the deputy, you could have just kidnapped his horse or something.

BANDIT. *(Returning to his attempt at tying a good knot.)* It's not that. I – I have to look unpredictable, it's scarier. My name is The Nefarious Bandit! I have to... uphold that name, and kidnapping the deputy's horse just looks like a grudge.

MARIBEL. And when the deputy comes anyway?

BANDIT. *(Improvising a plan.)* Then, I...I...I'll shoot him.

(He finishes the knot and turns away.)

MARIBEL. That would make for a tragic scene.

*(With the **BANDIT**'s back turned, **MARIBEL** removes the ropes to massage her wrists. The **BANDIT** notices and whips out his pistol.)*

(Slipping her hands back into the ropes, exasperated.)

Calm down! I'm not going to run anywhere.

BANDIT. *(Still nervous.)* Listen, it's been a long time since I've last done this, and I'm not feeling too good today. So, lay back down, I'm getting anxious.

MARIBEL. *(Completely calm, in control of the situation.)* Look. You've got to tie a bowline.

[Pronunciation note: "Bowline" rhymes with "stolen."]

*(She beckons the **BANDIT**. He steps forward to tie the knot again.)*

Up through the rabbit hole. Around the tree – No, no, other way. There. Back down through the – You got it!

BANDIT. Okay, looks good.

(He gets panicky again.)

Aagh! I've got to get my head! In! The! Game!

(He slaps his forehead with each exclaimed word.)

MARIBEL. Calm down!

BANDIT. *(Frantic.)* I only fumbled a little on a couple bank robberies, and suddenly I'm kicked out of the gang! I escaped half the county jails in the West with them, and they have the nerve to abandon me? Do you think I want to be back at square one, tying women to train tracks? No!

(He buries his head in his hands.)

How did I get here?

MARIBEL. *(Pulling one hand from the ropes for a comforting pat on the back.)* There, there.

BANDIT. How did – Stop doing that!

MARIBEL. Did you honestly think I gave you a working knot to tie me up?

BANDIT. *(Frustrated with himself.)* I didn't – I wasn't thinking about it!

(He squints into the distance, looking every which way.)

Where is he? Does the oh-so-important deputy have something better to do right now?

MARIBEL. I thought this wasn't about the deputy.

BANDIT. *(Cornered, backpedaling a little.)* Well, yeah, but I still need him to be here! You know, like a witness! Nobody's going to know it's me who killed you if there isn't a third-party...witness, you know? You're just going to be a...corpse, lying out in the middle of the desert!

MARIBEL. Thanks for that, by the way.

BANDIT. *(Oblivious to her comment.)* Those deputies! Nobody infuriates me more! They treat me like such... garbage, everywhere I go! Why are they like that?

MARIBEL. Maybe it has something to do with you murdering people? Or not, it's really anyone's guess.

BANDIT. Are you kidding? He NEEDS me. Do you get that? HE needs ME.

> *(He takes a breath, calms himself a little.)*

Listen, I don't need him. In fact, life would be easier for me if he wasn't around. I could do my job in peace.

MARIBEL. Peace.

BANDIT. It's an expression! Point is, I could get a whole lot more done without him. But if I'm not there? Then he loses everything. He needs crime to exist, he needs it to be prevalent, so that he has his...fame, his popularity, his sense of purpose. Without me, there's no fear, and without fear, there's no deputy. I mean, he may say he's doing his job for "moral rightness," but we all know it's just for his ego.

> *(Beat.)*

And the paycheck.

MARIBEL. Do you think he shouldn't be paid?

BANDIT. No, I don't even mind that. I just – I want a little credit, a little bit of thanks, for keeping him employed. That's all.

> *(He flops onto the ground. Beat. He begins to sob. Beat. **MARIBEL**, still tied up, inches toward him and does her best to console him.)*

(Through tears.) You know what?

> *(Beat.)*

He's a phony.

> *(Beat.)*

With his stupid ego.

> *(Beat.)*

And his...the money.

> *(He continues crying, more softly now. This goes on a bit too long for **MARIBEL**'s liking.)*

MARIBEL. *(Changing the topic.)* So, uh...why only women? What's the deal with that? It adds a layer of...creepiness, I have to say.

BANDIT. *(A little defensive.)* No, it's not about tying women to train tracks –

MARIBEL. And yet, it's only ever women.

BANDIT. That doesn't mean anything! I am absolutely comfortable tying men to railroad tracks too. You know, I've murdered over thirty men.

MARIBEL. How many did you kill by...by tying them to railroad tracks?

BANDIT. Well, none. But that doesn't mean I'm not –

MARIBEL. None! Not one!

BANDIT. But that doesn't mean I'm not totally open to the idea. It just, never really crossed my mind.

MARIBEL. Well, how do you ordinarily kill men?

BANDIT. Generally speaking?

MARIBEL. Yeah.

BANDIT. Well, um, I guess I shoot them. Usually in a robbery or heist...or shootout, a duel, though that's not very common. Shootouts are usually just for sheriffs, anyone in a powerful position.
(Realizing.) I've got it!

MARIBEL. What?

BANDIT. It's not a gender thing, it's occupation! You fight sheriffs in a...more formal way, to show you're a better sharpshooter than they are. To assert your dominance, you know.

MARIBEL. But you don't bother with the shopkeepers and bank tellers, and so on, because you don't have anything to prove...

BANDIT. I just need them out of the way, right. And women are tied to railroad tracks, or drowned in the water tower, or whatever, because our society perceives them as innocent...

MARIBEL. *(Excited.)* So, a particularly gruesome or brutal death is especially effective, since society views women as too pure for such an atrocity to be committed against them! It's symbolic! And you, of course, benefit from that, since it makes you look even more heartless and cruel!

> *(The reality of this finally sinks in for **MARIBEL**, who rediscovers that she is still facing imminent death. The **BANDIT** does not notice this yet.)*

BANDIT. I've never... I've never consciously thought about why we do it like that! It actually makes a lot of sense, though. Strike terror into the hearts of your enemies, while still abiding by a...specific, uh, code.

> *(He suddenly realizes the gravity of **MARIBEL**'s situation. He sits, a little guilty.)*

MARIBEL. You know, it isn't like this in other places. Back East, they don't have any of this, this whole bad-guy-and-woman-and-train-tracks thing. I mean, they have trains, of course, but –

BANDIT. Yeah, I get it.

> *(Beat.)*

You're from...back East?

MARIBEL. *(Hesitating a little, not a fan of talking about her personal life.)* Um, yeah, when I was younger. Getting an education together, working to be a schoolmarm in the untamed West...all that.

> *(A pause. She glances at the **BANDIT**. He is, for once, silent. She continues.)*

And getting away from it all, too. I loved the freedom, the newness, here. I was looking for...
(Glancing down at ropes, aware of the irony.) ...adventure.

> *(Beat.)*

And here I am, tied up again, just somewhere new.

BANDIT. Yeah, I get that.

MARIBEL. Moving? Somewhere new?

BANDIT. No, uh, being tied up. Metaphorically. To the code. And such.

> *(There is an awkward silence. Then the train whistle sounds again, a bit closer.)*

MARIBEL. *(Attempting to bring it up casually.)* So, uh, any chance you can let me just...go?

> *(A pause. The **BANDIT** considers. He's really tempted. But he shakes his head.)*

BANDIT. *(Sadly pointing his pistol.)* I'm sorry, but my whole career depends on this. I already let one go a couple years back, another woman on railroad tracks, coincidentally enough, and I'm still trying to make up for it, trying to show I'm...capable, you know, of following through.

MARIBEL. *(Seeing an opportunity.)* You...let her go? What, did you pity her or something?

BANDIT. No, no, she just...ran.

> *(Beat.)*

I didn't carry a pistol back then.

MARIBEL. I wouldn't tell anyone.

BANDIT. I can't...know that for sure.

MARIBEL. I'll just say I got lost, trying to find...a well or something.

BANDIT. A well?

MARIBEL. Look, I don't know. I'll come up with something better on the way back. Just...trust me, I'm not going to try to mess with you! You're The Nefarious Bandit! I know better than to try to one-up you!

BANDIT. I...I don't know. It seems risky.

MARIBEL. Don't talk to me about things being "risky" right now.

BANDIT. *(Suddenly cautious.)* Wait, wait, hold off on that for one moment.

MARIBEL. What? What is it?

BANDIT. The deputy is coming. Start crying for help.

MARIBEL. What? Why should I?

BANDIT. Because my reputation depends on it! Or because or else I'll shoot you in the head, whichever works for you! Go!

> (**MARIBEL** *stays silent. A very long pause. The* **BANDIT** *stops trying to be intimidating.*)

(*Pathetic.*) Please?

MARIBEL. (*Sighs, then yells and flails around.*) HELP, HELP, I'M OVER HERE! HELP MEEEE! PLEASE! ANYONE!

BANDIT. Nice! That's a...strong performance! I can really feel the...the pent-up terror!

MARIBEL. (*Sarcastic.*) Wow, really? I wonder where that came from. HELP ME! I'M ABOUT TO GET CRUSHED BY A TWO-HUNDRED-TON TRAIN! SOMEBODY GET OVER HERE NOW!

BANDIT. I've got to get in character! Come on, come on.

> (*He mentally prepares himself, then strikes a menacing pose. The* **DEPUTY** *enters heroically, performing immensely over-the-top.*)

DEPUTY. Have no fear, sweet Miss Maribel! I, the sheriff's mighty deputy, have come to your aid!

BANDIT. (*Fully becoming his villainous character.*) No, no, Deputy! You will be doing nothing of the sort! For this shall be my greatest crime, my most dazzling spectacle of carnage yet!

> (*Both the* **BANDIT** *and the* **DEPUTY** *point pistols at one another. Beat.*)

DEPUTY. (*Slowly lowering weapon.*) Lay down your pistol! Let's fight like men! And your dagger too, I know a crook like you must be hiding one.

BANDIT. Fair enough, Deputy. I'm nothing if not a good sport.

> (*The* **BANDIT** *steps away, setting down his pistol, then his dagger. He moves away to*

mentally prepare, waiting impatiently as **MARIBEL** *whispers privately to the* **DEPUTY**.)

MARIBEL. *(Whispering.)* Nice distraction.

DEPUTY. *(Loudly proclaimed, taking credit even though he has no idea what she means.)* Thank you, Miss Maribel!

MARIBEL. *(Whispering.)* Quiet! We don't want our friend here listening in.

DEPUTY. *(Whispering.)* Of course. Yes. What a despicable man.

> (**MARIBEL** *and the* **DEPUTY** *glance over. The* **BANDIT**, *noticing their gaze, hurriedly opens his jacket to reveal additional pistols. As per his word, he removes each one and lays them on the ground. He glances back at them, then continues to wait.)*

MARIBEL. *(Whispering as she unties herself.)* Okay, great. I've got the ropes. Let's go.

DEPUTY. *(Whispering.)* What?

MARIBEL. *(Whispering, gesturing with the loose ropes in her hands.)* The ropes. I got them off. We can leave now.

DEPUTY. *(Whispering, wording his response cautiously.)* Miss Maribel, you…you don't have to worry about those ropes. I will free you as soon as I apprehend this villain.

> (**MARIBEL** *and the* **DEPUTY** *again turn to check on the* **BANDIT**. *Rolling his eyes, he gives up some additional weaponry hidden somewhere on his person. Perhaps this includes a sawed-off shotgun, a billy club, brass knuckles, or some other device from the Old West. Again, the* **BANDIT** *turns back to check on them, and again, he waits.)*

MARIBEL. *(Whispering.)* No, the – the ropes are already off! I'm free! We can go!

DEPUTY. *(Whispering.)* But – Wait. Miss Maribel. I need to save you. From the bandit.

MARIBEL. *(Whispering.)* Yes.

DEPUTY. *(Whispering.)* I need to untie you. So you don't get run over by the train.

MARIBEL. *(Whispering.)* I know.

DEPUTY. *(Whispering.)* But – I mean – How can I untie you?

(There is a long pause.)

(Whispering.) You need to have the ropes on, so I can untie you.

MARIBEL. *(Almost to herself.)* I don't...even know what to say to that.

DEPUTY. *(Whispering.)* Look. I understand what you're trying to say.

(A pause. He attempts to rephrase.)

(Whispering.) We're on the same team here. I don't want the train to hit you.

MARIBEL. *(Whispering.)* Yeah. Me neither.

DEPUTY. *(Whispering.)* So. Could you...

(A pause.)

(Whispering.) I can't save you if –

*(**MARIBEL**, actually interrupting him with a silent death stare, ties herself up again. The **BANDIT** removes his cowboy hat and retrieves his final weapon. He turns to the **DEPUTY**.)*

BANDIT. All right! Time to settle the score!

*(The two circle around one another and begin to swing and parry fists. Meanwhile, **MARIBEL** slips her hands out of the ropes, grabs the dagger, cuts her ankles loose, and surreptitiously crawls for the gun, all during the following lines.)*

DEPUTY. I won't let you go through with your dastardly plans!

BANDIT. Not dastardly!

DEPUTY. Not...okay. Then, wicked!

BANDIT. No, no, you're not getting it.

DEPUTY. Your malicious –

BANDIT. With an "N." It starts with an "N."

DEPUTY. Nnnnnotorious?

> *(The **BANDIT** shakes his head.)*

Nnnnauseating.

> *(The **BANDIT** is impatient.)*

Nnnnot good!

BANDIT. Nefarious! My nefarious plans! I'm The Nefarious Bandit!

DEPUTY. Whatever you are! You are clearly a menace driven to the brink! Have no fear, young lass! I shall spare you from this monster's...

> *(Only now does he realize that **MARIBEL** is not on the tracks. Rather, she has acquired a pistol and stands, gun pointed at the **BANDIT**. The **DEPUTY** grins confidently. Beat. **MARIBEL** pivots. She shoots the **DEPUTY**. He crumples to the ground. There is a long pause. The **BANDIT** speaks, slowly.)*

BANDIT. You shot...him. Why?

> *(A long pause.)*

MARIBEL. He was a phony.

> *(A long pause.)*

BANDIT. But...uh, why not me?

> *(A long pause.)*

MARIBEL. You're...not.

> *(There is a very long pause. They gaze at each other. The **BANDIT** smiles.)*

BANDIT. *(Full of hope.)* And you're willing to ignore – I mean, you do understand, I've... Well, I've broken tons of laws, I've killed innocent people.

> *(He laughs.)*

I mean, you're willing to ignore that I fully intended to leave you here to die!

(A pause.)

MARIBEL. Fair point.

(She raises the pistol and, without emotion, shoots the **BANDIT**. *He topples. Now the only living person in the desert,* **MARIBEL** *stands, slowly lowering her gun, and thinks. There is a long silence. An approaching train sounds. Pocketing the pistol, she turns toward the tracks and sticks out her thumb, as a hitchhiker would, for a lift. Blackout.)*

End of Play

UMTYA (THE STRING)

Frances Louise Timberlake

UMTYA (THE STRING), by Frances Louise Timberlake of Troupe 3950 at the School for Creative and Performing Arts in Cincinnati, Ohio, was presented in a staged reading as part of the Thespian Playworks program at the 2018 International Thespian Festival on June 30, 2018. The production was directed by Phillip Moss, with dramaturgy by Judy GeBauer. The stage manager was William Higbie. The cast was as follows:

NOTU	Myah Lumford
UMA	Kelly Bolden
CHAIRMAN	Cleon Ony
ANODIWA	Casandra Sanches
COLONEL	Parker Medley
LIEUTENANT	John Eddy
SERGEANT	Shane Howell
KHATHU	EJ Service
CAPTAIN	Quinn Nehr
UTA	EJ Service
WOMAN	Aalanis Harrison
MTHANDAZO	Andrew Autry
BOY	Noah Tyler

CHARACTERS

NOTU [Noe-too] / **NOTUMATO** [Noe-too-ma-toe] – black girl, eleven years old

UMA [Oo-ma] – her mother, thirty years old

CHAIRMAN – middle-aged man

ANODIWA BORENG [On-oe-dee-wa Bore-ang] – black woman, fifty years old

COLONEL KHOMATSO [Koe-mot-soo] – white man, forty years old

LIEUTENANT GAMWE [Gom-way] – white man, sixty years old

SERGEANT VOLSTER – black man, thirty years old

KHATHU [Ku-thoo] – black man, mid-forties

CAPTAIN MAMASELA [Ma-ma-sel-a] – white man, late forties

UTA [Oo-ta] – Notu's father, mid-thirties

WOMAN – Notu years later, early forties

MTHANDAZO [Mu-thon-da-zoe] – black man, late thirties

BOY – black boy, four years old

AUTHOR'S NOTE

The Truth and Reconciliation Commission (TRC) was established by the Government of National Unity and led by Archbishop Desmond Tutu to help deal with the atrocities and injustices committed under apartheid in South Africa. Beyond the conventional police functions of upholding order and solving crime, the South African police employed counterinsurgency and intimidation tactics against anti-apartheid activists and critics of the white minority government. The conflict during apartheid resulted in violence and human rights abuses from all sides. No section of society escaped these abuses. In an open and transparent process, the TRC compiled a forensic record of apartheid-era human rights abuses. Testimonies revealed many cases of rape, torture, deaths in detention, political assassinations, and even human burnings. Yet the TRC's emphasis on amnesty and "restorative" justice – rather than "retributive" justice – was a product of the political need for societal stability and due legal process. The TRC helped reveal the worst excesses of apartheid and achieved a good measure of social reconciliation. Its lessons to the world for conflict resolution were profound. The process had a cathartic, healing effect that enabled the country to transcend the violence and acrimony of the apartheid years. The language used in this script is Xhosa, one of the eleven languages of South Africa. Xhosa is spoken by the Xhosa people, a Bantu ethnic group who live in south-central and southeastern regions of the country.

PRONUNCIATION GUIDE

eyoKwindla [ee-a-kwind-la] – March
eyeKhala [eye-kala] – July
uCanzibe [oo-kon-ze-bee] – May
eyeNkanga [eye-non-ga] – November
waarheid [var-heid] – truth
intombi [in-tome-be] – daughter
bakkie [ba-kee] – vehicle used to carry goods
uthando [oo-thon-doe] – love
Vlakplaas [vlock-plaz] – apartheid's death squad
eyoMnga [ee-a-mon-ga] – December
intliziyo [en-ti-zee-oe] – heart
Ndiyakuthanda [un-die-a-kooth-an-da] – I love you
tambuki [tam-boo-kee] – long prairie grass native to South Africa
marula [ma-roo-la] **tree** – woodland tree native to South Africa
Afrikaans [af-ri-konz] – official language of South Africa during apartheid

[The first scene is set in 1950 on the Bantu homeland at the beginning of apartheid. Imagine a shanty town with small farms in poor condition, but beyond this a field of tall grass and wildflowers on a cliff overlooking the ocean. Other scenes will be set in 1996 Cape Town, where characters give testimonies to the Human Rights Violations Committee, a component of the Truth and Reconciliation Commission established after apartheid. The time and setting will shift throughout the play. The rain daisy used throughout the story is a symbol of innocence and purity, so the meaningful act of placing the flower should be conveyed.]

(Lights up. **NOTU** *is sitting center stage with a rain daisy in her hand. Before she speaks, she places the daisy in front of her, as if laying it upon a grave.)*

NOTU. *(To audience.)* It's eyoKwindla, the month of the first fruits. It seems odd that you will only have one eyoKwindla when you're a certain age. We measure years of life with our birthdays. The beginning and end of a year is different from person to person. In the eyoKwindla of my eighth year, I had a bird. It was an ugly little thing with a tiny little head and big eyes. She had a broken wing because she had flown into a tree. She had these big round eyes, and she couldn't see the tree standing there right in front of her. I wonder if maybe she was rushing toward something. Maybe she had babies in a nest who needed to be fed. I wonder if maybe she was so worried about her hungry babies that she didn't see the tree there. I guess it doesn't matter much now, because her wing broke and she fell, and I found her like that. I didn't touch it because I didn't want to hurt it. It looked like she was hurting, and I didn't know whether to touch it or whether to just leave her there under the marula tree. I was eight, and the only thing I knew how to fix was my rag doll's head when it fell off, and even then I couldn't always fix that by myself. I'm eleven now, and I know how to fix many more things, but I didn't know what to do when I saw the bird with her broken wing, so I just picked her up and I let her breathe in my lap until I couldn't see her chest moving up and down anymore and her big round eyes were still open. Why do things die with their eyes open?

*(Lights shift. The **CHAIRMAN** is standing center stage.)*

CHAIRMAN. We are here because we need to see with open eyes what has passed through this chamber of horrors. There are no words strong enough to describe what is felt here. When truth has not been taught in the language they use, what word should then take its place? Waarheid, truth, truth. It doesn't roll off the tongue. It stays there like a pebble lodged between two boulders. It's like walls closing in, suffocating, and trapping. Truth is not justice, but justice must be done. Our stories need to be told, and only then can we consider moving on, moving forward.

*(Lights shift again onto **NOTU**. The **CHAIRMAN** places a rain daisy next to the other.)*

NOTU. Uma's going to have a baby. Her belly already looks like a big round mountain. Now, when she runs her fingers around on my back before I go to sleep, she has to stretch her arm past her belly. Sometimes she puts her hand underneath, like she's trying to hold the baby. I hope she did that for me before I was born. I hope she held me like that before she even saw me, because I think I would have liked it. I think I would have felt her arms even though I hadn't seen her yet, either. Uma sings her belly to sleep, too. I don't know what the baby looks like, but I know that it smiles when she sings. I wish I could sing like Uma. She sings so pretty. When she sings, it feels warm inside and outside it prickles. When she sings, I forget that I don't want to go to sleep and then I wake up in the morning and the last thing I remember is her voice.

> *(Lights shift. The* **CHAIRMAN** *is sitting stage right.* **ANODIWA BORENG** *enters and stands center stage. The* **CHAIRMAN** *turns and faces her.)*

CHAIRMAN. *(Looking at papers in front of him.)* This is Anodiwa Boreng. Her husband was murdered in 1977 along with three other young men. If you can, Mrs. Boreng, you may begin whenever you are ready.

ANODIWA. *(Her hands are shaking. She inhales.)* My husband was the president of the youth association. I remember how much they looked up to him. The youth were so disciplined. You could go around at night at that time, nobody would harm you, and we felt safe because of my husband. I would worry about him all the time, but you know I couldn't be upset with him because he was fighting for our rights and all he wanted was to win when all of our lives had been filled with losses.

CHAIRMAN. *(Looks to* **ANODIWA.**) You realize that it is actually quite possible for persons to come forward and admit to killing your husband and apply for amnesty. Would you like to know the name or names of those people who killed your husband?

ANODIWA. I need them to see me. I still feel so much pain, and my children feel so much pain, and we live with that. *(Breath.)* I don't understand how they live if they never open their eyes. They need to know that I'm just as real as the husband they took from me.

> *(Lights shift. The* **CHAIRMAN** *leads* **ANODIWA** *to the flowers. She places another daisy near the other two. She exits. The* **CHAIRMAN** *returns to his former position.* **NOTU** *is standing now.)*

NOTU. I will begin school again when the sun begins to take long strolls in the sky. That's what Uma says. She says that seasons change because the sun will sometimes get tired of watching us. He goes away in the winter, and then when he misses us again, he will return. I don't think I would like to be the sun. I think it would be lonely, always watching but never touching.

(**UMA** *enters. She sees* **NOTU** *and smiles.*)

UMA. You've been out here for a long time.

NOTU. I like being outside. It smells good.

UMA. What does it smell of here?

NOTU. *(Thinking before she speaks.)* Like the sea and new air and growing.

UMA. Aren't you bored out here all alone?

NOTU. I like doing things by myself, and sometimes I have more fun when I don't have to talk to anyone. I can think about things and say things that don't make sense to anyone else. But when I feel alone, I talk to the sky and it hears everything.

UMA. *(Beginning to exit.)* You make sure to come home before it gets dark, and don't get too close to the cliff.

(*She exits. Lights shift.* **NOTU** *looks at the flowers.* **KHATHU** *is already onstage, sitting just where Anodiwa had been.*)

KHATHU. We went on holiday to a game farm near Messina. We were in the bakkie. All of us pushed up against each other. The back wheel on the right, the exact spot where my eighteen-month-old girl was sitting, struck a landmine. We were immediately in flames. I imagine some time passed, because when I came to I saw my brother was lying on his steering wheel. His hair burning, blood spouting from his forehead. He was still breathing. I climbed out, and right behind the vehicle, I found my wife and his wife. Both killed outright. Their faces weren't their faces anymore. I searched further. I came upon my nephew, who had some life in him. I went to my brother and said, the child is still alive but severely maimed and burnt. His father asked, there on the scene, to let his child go and then he too died. I saw my daughter. She was lying still and had no eyes, but she was looking right at me. I buried my wife and I buried my girl and the next day my brother and his family. Sometimes I sit for days. I simply sit.

CHAIRMAN. May we adjourn for ten minutes, please?

> *(Lights shift.* **NOTU** *is at home now.* **UMA** *is doing household chores, maybe cleaning the floor.* **NOTU** *is sitting on the floor, playing with her rag doll.)*

NOTU. *(Looking up at* **UMA.***)* Does it hurt?

UMA. *(Preoccupied.)* Does what hurt?

NOTU. Does your belly hurt?

UMA. *(Chuckling, she has slowed her pace, now listening to* **NOTU.***)* No, intombi. It just feels heavy.

NOTU. Is it uncomfortable?

UMA. Sometimes, but I just remember that it only feels heavy because that's how much I love it.

NOTU. *(Playing with her doll's hair.)* Do you know what? I think I would like a sister.

UMA. Oh? And why not a brother?

NOTU. I think a sister would like me more. She'd like the things I like and I'd show her how to do her hair and how to smell the fruit before you buy it and how to talk. A boy wouldn't listen to me or want to play with me. Boys say mean things.

UMA. What kinds of things?

> *(Beat.)*

NOTU. At school, they call me ugly.

UMA. Boys tell you you're ugly?

NOTU. *(Turning away.)* Yes. They say that my eyes are too big for my face, and my legs are too short, and my arms are too long.

UMA. *(Crossing to* **NOTU** *and sitting next to her.)* Can I tell you something? There are some fruits that have bright colors, but when you bite into them they are bitter and inedible. Then there are fruits that have no color, or are covered in spikes, and for a long time no one wants that fruit, but those who are clever enough to take a chance on the simple spiky fruit will taste the sweetest juice they have ever tasted and never look at the bright fruit again.

NOTU. It doesn't matter what's inside if no one ever wants to pick the ugly fruit.

UMA. There will always be someone. But the spiky fruit also knows that inside it's sweeter than the bright fruit, and sometimes knowing is enough.

NOTU. What if I'm ugly forever?

UMA. *(Kneels in front of* **NOTU** *and cups her face.)* You could never be ugly, Notu. Don't ever say that again. Do you understand?

NOTU. Yes.

UMA. Give me your hand.

> *(She places* **NOTU***'s hand on her belly, and* **NOTU** *jumps back when she finally feels the kick.)*

That's the baby kicking.

NOTU. Why is the baby kicking you? Is the baby angry?

UMA. I think excited. Happy and warm and ready to see you.

NOTU. Did I kick, too?

UMA. You kicked so hard that I could feel each of your little toes. You wanted to see everything, you never slept.

NOTU. I wish I could remember what it was like before I was born. I wish I never had to forget anything.

UMA. Sometimes forgetting is good. We have to forget things because they aren't important enough to remember and leave room for the big memories.

NOTU. What if we forget all the happy things?

UMA. Then we have to find new happy things. But you're lucky. You don't need to look far to find the happy things. You have so much love from your family and so many thoughts, and you can see things that other people won't let their eyes see.

NOTU. Uta says that I ask too many questions.

UMA. Well, there are times when it's more important to listen than ask questions.

NOTU. I don't think I like listening very much.

UMA. Listening is just as important as seeing. Listen the same way that you see things so easily. Listen to people. Listen to rain and the wind. Everything has something to say.

(Lights shift. **KHATHU** *and the* **CHAIRMAN** *resume their dialogue.)*

KHATHU. I live alone, sir. I hear silence. There are many days that I open my mouth and find that no sound escapes, because I don't speak most days. I don't believe in souls, sir. I don't believe that we go anywhere after death, and I don't believe that my family is watching over me and listening to me while I speak, so I do not talk to them. It is much easier for me that way, because I know that they are gone. I do not hold onto them like a balloon that a child ties around his wrist. However, just because I know they are gone does not mean that I don't curse myself in the morning when I realize that I have gone through the day before without thinking of them once.

CHAIRMAN. What do you hope to achieve today?

KHATHU. I wanted to tell my story. My daughter's story, my wife's story. My family's story. I think I had to. I don't expect anyone to admit to planting the landmine. There are hundreds just like them: people who have lost their loved ones too.

(Lights shift. **KHATHU** *exits and places his flower.* **UMA** *and* **NOTU** *resume their dialogue.)*

UMA. *(Covers **NOTU**'s eyes with her hands.)* You don't always need to keep your eyes open.

NOTU. It's dark.

UMA. Yes, I know. Try to listen.

NOTU. *(Pausing to listen before she speaks.)* Your voice sounds different. Not louder, but it feels deeper. I feel it in here. *(Indicates her chest.)* And I can feel air like it's in my back.

UMA. *(Kneels in front of **NOTU** and removes her hands.)* You have beautiful eyes, intombi, but your eyes can't tell you everything. Those boys at school can't tell you what you are just by looking.

NOTU. *(Places hands over her mother's eyes.)* What do you feel?

UMA. I feel you. And I feel the baby. And I feel your uta, even though he is not here right now.

NOTU. Uta is never here.

> *(**UMA** gently pulls **NOTU**'s hands from her face and turns toward her. Still sitting, she brings **NOTU** into her lap.)*

UMA. He works, intombi. He's working so we can live in this house and so you can eat and I can go to the doctor. And, you know, when he does come home you can give him a big hug.

NOTU. I don't want him to hug me.

UMA. Notumato, please don't say things like that. Uta tries for you and for me, even though he sees things every day that make him want to give up.

NOTU. I don't love him the same as I love you.

UMA. It would hurt him very much to hear you say that. Do you not see how fathers don't always come home like your uta does? There are little girls just like you down the street who ask their mothers when their fathers are going to walk through the door again, and the mothers don't know what to say except soon. And when soon doesn't come, the little girls stop waiting at the window and forget what their fathers look like.

NOTU. I remember what he looks like.

*(Lights shift. **WOMAN** is sitting with the **CHAIRMAN**.)*

WOMAN. I remember what he looked like. I remember every detail, every crease in his face when he smiled, and the little curve on the bridge of his nose. I remember his hands and his shoulders. His shoulders were always so strong. Stronger than mine. He was stronger than me.

CHAIRMAN. You lost your son and now you're here. That's strength, too.

WOMAN. *(Smiles slightly and closes her eyes as if to hold back tears.)* On that day, I was at work. I heard the people saying that there was a boy who had been shot, but I just ignored that. The news bulletin would be on at six o'clock. I switched on the television. As I was still watching the news I saw Christoph. I knew it was him because he was wearing the shirt I bought him when he graduated school. That was such a happy day.

(Beat.)

He was on the ground and his eyes were open and his mouth was open. There were police officers taking pictures of him, touching him with their gloves like he was dirty. They called him a terrorist. They never used his name, they just called him a terrorist. They had to take his body away, and he was being pulled with the rope that was tied around his waist. His body was being pulled. I saw my child on TV and nobody had come to tell me that he was dead.

(Long pause.)

Now I think that maybe I was lucky. I know what happened to my son. I can't imagine the pain of the mothers whose sons just never came home. It's so lonely when you lose a child. You don't feel anything after a while and all you can do is think about what he could have become. Those mothers also have to imagine how and why he can't become anything, though.

CHAIRMAN. Every mother has suffered the pain of childbirth, and to lose the child you love is very painful. It's a wound that does not heal.

(Lights shift. **NOTU**'s *thought continues.)*

NOTU. He has a hard face, and sometimes when he talks he puts his hand on his head and scrunches up his eyes.

UMA. What about his smile?

NOTU. I was going to talk about that. He has a huge smile and you can see all of his teeth, even the ones in the back. He claps his hands when he laughs and stomps his feet, it's like thunder, but not as scary.

UMA. Tell me about his hands.

NOTU. His hands are bigger than mine and yours together. He said his fingers got stuck in a jar once when he was trying to steal some jam before dinner. He had wanted it so much that he put all his fingers in and he had to stretch his hands so far to get them out. But I don't think that's true.

UMA. Stories don't have to be true.

(Lights shift.)

WOMAN. The worst crime was that they didn't help you heal. There was the time I went to the court for my son's case. The magistrate said nobody was to blame because the police were defending themselves. The whole time I was there in court, they spoke Afrikaans and they never translated for me. I felt so small. They enjoyed themselves, laughing at me because it was easy for them and impossible for me. They wouldn't let me get justice for my son. I wonder whether they still laugh, now that the mothers they laughed at have a voice that will be heard in every language.

*(**WOMAN** places her flower. Lights out. Lights up on **NOTU**, sitting center stage just as she was in the opening sequence.)*

NOTU. *(Holding a flower.)* Uta came back in eyeKhala. He had bruises on his face, but he wouldn't let Uma see.

One of his eyes didn't open. He smelled funny. He said I was taller, and I said he had just been gone for a long time. Uma didn't like that I said so, but Uta smiled and he laughed, but he didn't clap, or stomp his feet, and it didn't sound like thunder. It sounded like empty tins knocking together. He laughs like that more now. He said he's staying for a little while, maybe three days, but I wish he'd go back to the city. He didn't remember where Uma puts the bowls or where the toilet was. I want him to leave because Uma looks sad. Uta didn't want to feel the baby kick.

(She begins ripping leaves from the stem.)

He spends a lot of time outside, and Uma says it's because he doesn't see outside as much in the city because he works in the mines, where there's no sun. I don't think that's why he goes outside, though, but Uma won't let me tell her why. She says I shouldn't talk about Uta, because it's not kind. Is it unkind if I still think it?

(She rolls the leaves between her fingers.)

Last year in uCanzibe, Uta came back and he said that we were going to do something secret. I couldn't tell Uma because it was going to be all our own. At night, he took me outside and we lay down on our backs in the tambuki grass with our knees poking out, looking so far away, and he told me to look up and I'd see the stars hanging from the sky by cords. I asked him why I couldn't see the cords, and he said because they were spirits who didn't want to be born. The spirits had to hold the stars for the people and the animals, because that was their job. He said his job was to carve rock when he was here, but when his spirit left his body he hoped he would be able to hold a star right above our house, so he could see me and Uma. And he held my hand, because sometimes when older people talk about leaving their families they get sad. When I get sad I hold Uma's hand, and maybe that's what Uta was doing. I didn't know if I wanted him to hold my hand, but I let him, anyway, and we fell asleep on our backs, with our knees up in the tambuki grass.

(She lets the stem fall to the ground.)

I don't think Uta wants to hold my hand anymore.

(Lights shift. The **CHAIRMAN** *is the only character onstage.)*

CHAIRMAN. This is very difficult. Bringing you here to talk about your pain and having to watch you re-experience the pain that you felt in dealing with the tragedy of your loss. These are the stories that we want our children to remember. We want them to remember that we paid a price in order for us to be free today. We say that we hope that the Lord will support and strengthen you, because we don't have any more words to comfort you.

(Lights out. Lights up on the **CHAIRMAN**. *He is holding a Bible and standing at the podium, addressing the public. There are five chairs onstage, behind which are* **COLONEL KHOMATSO, CAPTAIN MAMASELA, LIEUTENANT GAMWE, SERGEANT VOLSTER,** *and* **MTHANDAZO**. *Lights up on the* **OFFICERS**, *who step out from behind their chairs. The* **CHAIRMAN** *is now addressing the men onstage.)*

You have come here seeking amnesty for your crimes. Understand that the families who will witness your testimony may decide whether you are granted amnesty or not. It is critical that you tell only the truth at this moment.

(Extending the Bible forward to each man.)

Do you swear that the evidence you are giving is the truth and nothing but the truth, so help you God?

(Each **OFFICER** *raises their right hand.)*

OFFICERS. Yes.

(They drop their right hands.)

(The COLONEL steps forward, holding a folder with papers, while the other four men take their seats. The other men do not acknowledge the COLONEL. They should appear as if they are not witnessing his testimony, as if they are not in the same place in time. The CHAIRMAN takes a seat. ANODIWA, KHATHU, and WOMAN enter. They have headsets that are transmitting a translation of the testimony. ANODIWA looks up at the COLONEL.)

CHAIRMAN. Colonel Khomatso, I understand you have come here today to admit to the killing of Andile Boreng.

COLONEL. I brought papers. They document my instructions to monitor Andile Boreng, as he was a known ANC member, an anti-apartheid activist.

(He hands a folder to the CHAIRMAN, who opens it and begins to read through the papers. He crosses to his chair and sits.)

I was told by my superiors that I was to find the home of Mr. Boreng, but they didn't say anything more. When I found his address, I gave it to them. Then they told me to watch the house and record his movements. I did this for a week. I slept when he slept. I woke when he woke, and I followed him to work every morning. I was discreet. He never saw me, and at the time I was very proud of this. When I reported back, they told me that they had enough to prove he was planning a coup. I told them that I hadn't heard of this, but they said that they had proof from other intelligence officers. They told me to kill him.

(The CHAIRMAN sets down the papers, turns his attention to the COLONEL.)

CHAIRMAN. And you murdered Mr. Boreng because you were instructed to?

COLONEL. Yes. I followed him home. I went inside his house.

(Beat.)

COLONEL. I walked up behind him and I shot him in the back of the head with a .22 caliber gun. There was brain matter and blood on the wall in front of him, so I took a dish towel from the kitchen and wiped it off of the walls. I don't know why I did that.

> *(Beat.)*

I put his body into the back of a truck that was waiting. There were other officers with me, because we had to find the three others. I told them to drive away quickly. I didn't want to be there when the wife got home.

> *(**ANODIWA** turns away from him. She is not crying. The **COLONEL** places his flower. Lights shift to **NOTU**. She is wearing a sweater and is carrying a small blanket.)*

NOTU. EyeNkanga is cold, so Uma makes me wear this, but it's itchy. I'd rather be cold than itchy. Uta made me go outside because Uma had the baby today. It's too cold for him to be born, so when he came out his eyes were closed. Uma was crying, but I think when it warms up he will open his eyes. No one wants to be awake when it's cold. I take long sleeps a lot when it's cold outside.

> *(Lights shift to the men once again. The **LIEUTENANT** should seem self-assured, arrogant. The **SERGEANT** appears more on edge. They do not acknowledge each other. As before, they should appear as if they are in separate times, giving their own interpretation of the crimes committed.)*

CHAIRMAN. We have Lieutenant Gamwe and Sergeant Volster here with us now. They will be applying for amnesty for the killing of three black students and the disposal of their bodies along with that of Mr. Boreng.

LIEUTENANT. *(Clearing his throat.)* Our duties are made very clear from the beginning. We are trained to prevent resistance and rebellion.

CHAIRMAN. And you believe the actions of these four men required such violence?

LIEUTENANT. As I said, we have been trained to react to rebellion with force appropriate to the act.

CHAIRMAN. But you are then saying that the killing was justified?

LIEUTENANT. That was how we were trained.

CHAIRMAN. I am interested then to know why you have come forward. You are not admitting that you did anything wrong, but you are maintaining that if you had done something wrong, then you are applying for amnesty. That remains your position?

LIEUTENANT. I make it clear in my amnesty application. I am saying I am sorry that I took a life and I am asking for amnesty for it. It has happened and it is past, and I think one should just try and prevent this kind of thing happening again. I am, I believe, attempting to explain that we were doing what we had been taught. Mr. Chairman, before I retired I put my gun in a leather purse and I took it everywhere, even when I went to the toilet. Our training was to fear the things that threatened the government and to take measures to subdue these fears at any cost. But I feared everything. I still carry the purse with me. There is no gun in it. It is out of habit, but it's the only thing that makes me feel...safe.

(Lights shift. The **SERGEANT** *stands. The* **LIEUTENANT** *sits.)*

CHAIRMAN. This committee recognizes the truth, Sergeant. Begin.

SERGEANT. There were times when I was told to bring people to headquarters and hand them over to the men whose names and faces I could never forget. They would take the accused persons away, many would never return. I don't know how many men's lives I helped end. We were trained to not remember their names. There were thousands and no one knew their names.

(Lights shift.)

NOTU. I don't know his name. Uma said I could name the baby when it came, but I think she forgot because she won't tell me what his name is. Uta said I should stop asking questions, but it doesn't matter because no one will answer them anyway. I think Uma is sick. She stays in her room even when it's light outside. She tells me to go to Mrs. Sangoma's house a lot. I told her yesterday that I didn't want to go, because I wanted to stay with her and she didn't like that. She yelled. Uma used to say that she didn't like to yell because her uta yelled too much. I don't think she sleeps now. She says she's tired. This morning I went into her room to wake her up and the sheets were wet. Her dress was wet, the bed smelled bad. She didn't want to move, so I had to pull her up. I gave her a bath and she didn't look at me. I took her sheets off the bed and I washed them, but they still smell. I think Uma is sick.

*(Lights shift. Both the **LIEUTENANT** and the **SERGEANT** are standing. They are referencing the same event, but their stories do not match up. Their dialogue alternates quickly.)*

LIEUTENANT. They were in a garage, talking.

SERGEANT. I started out in the truck. Colonel Khomatso and Lieutenant Gamwe got out and headed toward a garage.

LIEUTENANT. I took my gun and I shot the first man, then the second. Then Sergeant Volster shot the third.

SERGEANT. They were gone for a while, so I got out of the truck and I went toward the garage. They had metal pipes in their hands and they kept hitting them over and over again. They told me to come closer. They told me to ask one of them to name other ANC members. He said he would rather die.

LIEUTENANT. They died instantly.

SERGEANT. They told me to hit him, then to kick him, then to shoot him. I think he was already dead before I shot him. The other two were already dead when I got there. They died one by one, but they all had the same look in their eyes, like they had seen God's face and were at peace. I wonder if I'll ever see God's face, after what I've done.

LIEUTENANT. We loaded them into the truck.

SERGEANT. We dragged their bodies to the truck and threw them on top of the one that was already there.

LIEUTENANT. We drove to a field by this river. We unloaded the bodies.

SERGEANT. We put their bodies on a pile of wood. I poured diesel over them and the wood. My superior lit the fire.

LIEUTENANT. My subordinate lit a fire. The bodies were burnt entirely after approximately six to eight hours. The next morning, we gathered the ash together and put it into black bags. They emptied the bags in the river.

SERGEANT. We had the instructions to destroy all evidence of what we had done. I was told to empty the bags into the river. I watched it all get swept away.

LIEUTENANT & SERGEANT. We left.

(The LIEUTENANT and SERGEANT place their flowers. Lights shift to NOTU and UMA. NOTU's head is rested on her mother's shoulder. UMA's appearance has changed. She is expressionless and her hair and clothes are more unkempt than they were previously.)

NOTU. Uma, can you sing to me?

UMA. No, intombi.

NOTU. Uta says you're not feeling well. He told me to leave you alone.

UMA. He's just trying to make me feel better. I won't make you sick.

NOTU. I don't want to listen to him anyway. I think he's just upset that I like you more. He's mean and angry. He doesn't work anymore, but he's never home. He can't be my father if he's never here.

(Lights shift. The COLONEL, LIEUTENANT, and SERGEANT are standing. The CHAIRMAN turns

to **ANODIWA**, *who removes her headset. He turns to the men.*)

CHAIRMAN. In the case of Colonel Khomatso, amnesty has been denied. In the cases of Lieutenant Gamwe and Sergeant Volster, amnesty has been denied.

(*Lights shift. The* **COLONEL**, **LIEUTENANT**, **SERGEANT**, *and* **ANODIWA** *exit. They each place a flower as they exit.*)

UMA. (*Turns back to* **NOTU**.) Intombi, do you know what your name means?

NOTU. No.

UMA. Your name, Notumato, means beautiful at birth. To me it means that you don't need to see something to love it. You can love your uta even though you aren't able to see him every day.

NOTU. Is that what you do? When you think about him, is that what you do?

UMA. I did see him. I saw him for a second, but I loved him before that, too.

NOTU. I think I would have liked him. I don't think I would have cared if he didn't want to play with me or do the things that I wanted.

(**UMA** *places a hand on her abdomen. Then she crouches in front of* **NOTU**, *placing her hands on her child's knees.*)

UMA. Close your eyes.

(**NOTU** *closes her eyes quickly.*)

Can you feel that string, intombi? It's vibrating with every breath that we take and with every life that has been taken. There is magic, like when you were born and you saw me for the first time, and then there is pain, like when your brother couldn't look at me for the first time.

(*Beat.*)

I want you to feel everything. And when you grow up, you might find that there are people who won't care if they cause you pain, but you must show them that you love them even if you can't see any good. Can you do that for me?

(**NOTU** *opens her eyes and nods.*)

NOTU. I'm sorry that he isn't here.

UMA. I know.

NOTU. I'm sorry that Uta isn't here, too.

UMA. I know.

NOTU. Do you know what?

UMA. What?

NOTU. I think that you're going to be all right. You're always all right.

(*Lights shift. Now the* **CAPTAIN** *stands.*)

CHAIRMAN. Captain Mamasela, could you please begin by explaining your position on the police force.

CAPTAIN. Between 1973 and 1989 I was a Vlakplaas operative. I was responsible for undercover operations. My job was to infiltrate anti-apartheid organizations and report names of leaders and the most involved activists.

CHAIRMAN. And were you also responsible for planting landmines?

CAPTAIN. Sometimes I was told that no names were needed and my fellow officers and I were told to plant landmines. They were intended for military purposes, but they didn't have names on them. We may have killed hundreds of innocent people, and I will never know.

CHAIRMAN. And you believe you planted the landmine that took the lives of two children and three adults?

CAPTAIN. I have applied for amnesty because this is a war crime. Apartheid was a war on people I didn't know and didn't care to learn about. I may as well have killed those children and those adults. As an officer, I was taught that the lives of the dead shouldn't mean anything to us. I was taught that the lives of the living were the only ones that mattered. I am taking responsibility for the killing of these families and asking for amnesty because

I need to feel I have some chance of forgiveness when I finally stand in front of God.

> (*Lights shift to* **NOTU**. *The* **CAPTAIN** *places his flower. He sits.*)

NOTU. It's colder now. EyoMnga brings cold that stings and thorn trees who have lost their leaves that sting even more. The wind likes to moan and the sun hides behind clouds that make the sky gray. EyoMnga is not happy, but Uma is getting better. She is getting out of her bed and eating. She will not look at me, but sometimes she smiles when I bring her food or a blanket. I told her that I would get really good at reading when I go back to school. I want to read her stories that make her laugh. I think that will make her start looking at me again.

> (**UMA** *enters. She crosses down to stand on a cliff.*)

There was one time when I was younger that she took me to see the doctor. We walked for a long time to get to the doctor because she is so far away. Uma told me that she has to be in the middle, so that everyone is the same distance away and can come to her. It was hot, and when we got there, there was a long line that was far away from the doctor's house. I told Uma that I was hungry and she gave me half of an orange, and when there was only one piece left, she gave it to me.

> (**UMA** *rests her hand on her abdomen. She is facing the audience.*)

We waited in line for a long time, too. When it got dark, a man with light skin came out and told us that we all needed to go home. He told us to come back earlier if we wanted to see the doctor, but Uma said that we couldn't go again for a while because she had to begin the harvest and I had to go to school. The man said he was sorry, but he didn't seem that sorry. Uma said he just wanted us to go home, so he could go home. We had to turn around and we had to walk back, and it was dark, and Uma sang and she looked at me and she stopped singing and we stopped walking. And we stood like that for a little while and waited until the sun had been chased away by the moon, until the spirits came out with the stars on cords and let them fall into the sky. I squeezed her hand, and she squeezed back.

>   (**UMA** *looks down, as if seeing what lies beneath the cliff.*)

After that, I asked Uma what uthando was. We started walking again and she told me that it was everything that was in her heart and everything that was in my heart. I told her that sometimes my heart, my intliziyo, hurt and she said it was because sometimes uthando can be too heavy and when we're older, we get stronger and it doesn't hurt as much.

>   (**UMA** *closes her eyes and looks up. The palms of her hands are open to the audience.*)

I don't think Uma's old enough yet, because it's still too heavy for her to carry all the time. Even when she is lying in her bed or sitting, it hurts. I know that if it's too heavy for her, it will be too heavy for me. She's stronger than me. I don't ask her a lot of questions now. She needs to rest because she gets tired from carrying her intliziyo around all the time. Sometimes I bring her things and if she's awake, she smiles, but she's not awake much now.

>   (**UMA** *looks at* **NOTU**, *but* **NOTU** *still doesn't acknowledge her mother's presence.* **BOY** *enters behind* **UMA**. *He takes her hand and he leads her upstage out of the light, and they exit together. Lights out. Lights up on* **NOTU**, *now in a spotlight, standing center stage.*)

Uma jumped when it was raining. Rain has a way of making people see things with sad eyes. Maybe because it feels like tears. Tears all around you and they don't stop for anyone.

*(Lights shift. The **CAPTAIN** stands. The **CHAIRMAN** turns to **KHATHU**, who removes his headset. He turns to the **CAPTAIN**.)*

CHAIRMAN. In the case of Captain Mamasela, amnesty has been denied.

*(Lights out. The **CAPTAIN** and **KHATHU** exit, each placing flowers before they leave. Lights up. **UTA** enters. **NOTU** is kneeling on the ground, staring blankly into the audience. He stands apart from her. He is uncomfortable.)*

UTA. It's dark, Notumato. You're going to have to come in now.

NOTU. It doesn't feel good in there when she's not here, and it doesn't feel good when you're here. Uma would have told me I shouldn't say so, but it's true. She's gone and you're here, and it's going to stay that way.

UTA. Yes, that's how it's going to stay.

*(Moving closer to **NOTU**. He hesitates before he speaks, trying to think of the right words.)*

When I'm sad I look at the stars. I can still feel the rocks in my belly, but they're not as heavy. Do you remember what I told you about the stars, Notu?

NOTU. *(Lying.)* No.

UTA. *(Knows she is lying.)* I told you that the stars were hung from cords by the spirits that live in the sky. I told you that the spirits were souls who didn't want to be born. I didn't tell you that some are also souls who didn't want to live.

NOTU. Uma?

UTA. *(Nodding.)* And your brother.

NOTU. Why didn't she want to stay for me? I'm still here.

UTA. She was tired of carrying her intliziyo. It was so full of you and your brother. She was so tired. But I think she can carry it now. She is so strong now that she has flown up into the sky and now she can hold her own star, too.

(They both lie back with their knees sticking up. **NOTU** *reaches out to hold* **UTA**'s *hand. They hold hands. Lights shift.* **MTHANDAZO** *stands.)*

CHAIRMAN. What were your instructions?

MTHANDAZO. The words that were used were that he should be eliminated. But the boy approached us with his arms in the sky.

CHAIRMAN. Could you please show us how he raised his arms?

*(***MTHANDAZO*** stands up, holding his arms raised in the manner assumed when wishing to surrender.)*

And is it correct that this person who approached you at no time attempted to shoot you?

MTHANDAZO. He never tried to shoot us or even to reach for his firearm. I shot him in the head, I shot him while he was lying on his back.

CHAIRMAN. Would you please tell us, why have you applied for amnesty?

MTHANDAZO. I wanted to let this thing out. I'm a black man. For me, it's more because I had to face my black brothers and sisters. And that's a daily thing. Every day the others are going to the bar with their white friends. I have to go to my black brothers and sisters.

*(***MTHANDAZO*** stands and crosses with his chair downstage. He sits. The* **CHAIRMAN** *stands and crosses with his chair downstage. He places it across from* **MTHANDAZO** *and then crosses to* **WOMAN**.*)*

CHAIRMAN. This is the first time you will meet the person who killed your child. You can say whatever you are wanting to say or to ask, with our support.

*(***WOMAN*** removes her headset and crosses to the empty chair by* **MTHANDAZO** *and sits.)*

MTHANDAZO. My name is Mthandazo. I know that it is painful for you to be faced with a person who has done you wrong and to talk to him. I have done evil things here on Earth. I ask your forgiveness from the bottom of my heart.

WOMAN. When he raised his hands and said he was surrendering, you shot him while he was in the act of surrendering. You shot my child. So how do you feel now? And the day when you saw it on that video, how did you feel?

MTHANDAZO. I feel, I felt bad.

WOMAN. I wonder, how much worse do you think I feel?

MTHANDAZO. I was forced to do what I did. It was a situation where I didn't know whether I was coming or going. I had to take orders. I was told, I didn't do the telling.

WOMAN. But we are your own people. When you look at that day, what does your conscience say to you? When you really look at it, Mthandazo?

MTHANDAZO. I don't know what to say. I have hurt you.

WOMAN. It is so painful for me. No matter what he had done, my child was thrown away like a dog. They dragged him with that rope, they dragged him. I just cannot bear this thought. We mothers who have had our children taken away from us too early are just sitting here. We don't have work, we don't have anything. That is our pain.

*(Lights shift back to the place where **NOTU** and **UTA** are lying.)*

NOTU. I forgive you.

UTA. I think we are going to be all right, Notumato.

*(Lights shift back to **WOMAN** and **MTHANDAZO**.)*

WOMAN. Doesn't the name Mthandazo mean prayer?

MTHANDAZO. Yes.

WOMAN. I see what your name means, although I don't know whether you follow it or not. You and Christoph are the same age, except my child will never wake up again. You will. You do. It is very painful for me to hold this wound against you. God will be the judge. My uma believed that there is a string that connects you and me and my son and everyone else. We feel each other. We feel each breath, each life, even those that have been taken. So, there is no place for throwing the stones I feel in my belly every day at you, even though you did those things. Because I want to get rid of this burden I am carrying inside, so that I can feel at peace. As best I can, I forgive you, Mthandazo.

*(Lights out. Lights up. The **CHAIRMAN** is the only character onstage.)*

CHAIRMAN. If you close your eyes and you imagine a future for this country that is good and light and safe, that is hope. If you are able to imagine a country where mothers don't have to check the morgue when their child has not come home from school and a country where the police carry out laws that don't take away human rights but encourage them, then that is hope. When I close my eyes, I see this, but there are things that I can't get out of my mind too. Things that don't belong in our country now and certainly won't belong in our country fifty years from now. I know hope, but I also know hopelessness, and both have their place in ensuring that this never happens again.

*(Lights out, except for one spotlight that remains on **NOTU**, who is holding all the flowers that have been placed by each of the characters throughout the play.)*

NOTU. When I felt alone, I used to talk to the sky. Now, I talk to Uma's star. I talk to her about Uta and school, and the flowers that change every season. I told Uma that I heard Uta crying last night. I think Uma would tell me that Uta gets lonely too sometimes and so I should try to be nice to him. I told him I forgive him for not coming home, because he's here now and I know he won't leave again. I can feel it when he holds my hand. It feels the same as when Uma used to hold both sides of my face and say, "Ndiyakuthanda, Ndiyakuthanda, I love you." I miss Uma, but I know that she's holding her star on the same string that's holding me and everything else.

End of Play

www.ingramcontent.com/pod-product-compliance
Lightning Source LLC
Chambersburg PA
CBHW051408290426
44108CB00015B/2197